MAKING MEDIEVAL MANUSCRIPTS

MAKING MEDIEVAL MANUSCRIPTS

Christopher *de'* Hamel

BODLEIAN
LIBRARY
PUBLISHING

First published in 2018 by the Bodleian Library
Broad Street, Oxford OX1 3BG

www.bodleianshop.co.uk

2nd impression 2021

ISBN: 978 1 85124 468 3

Previously published as *Scribes and Illuminators*
by the British Museum Press, 1992

Cover design by Dot Little at the Bodleian Library

Designed and typeset by Laura Parker in Enigma 2 in 10.5 pt on 15.1 pt font

Printed and bound by 1010 International Ltd. on 157gsm Oji matt art paper

British Library Catalogue in Publishing Data
A CIP record of this publication is available from the British Library

FRONTISPIECE (p. 4): Saint Mark shown in the Ranshofen Gospels,
writing a manuscript inspired by the lion, which is his symbol in art.
He holds a quill pen and a knife, and there is an inkhorn in the edge of his
desk. (MS Canon. Bibl. Lat. 60, Austria (Salzburg), dated 1178).

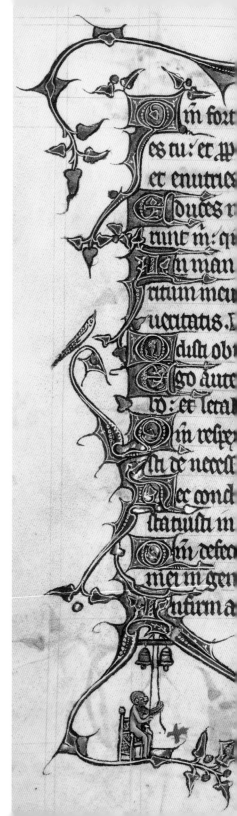

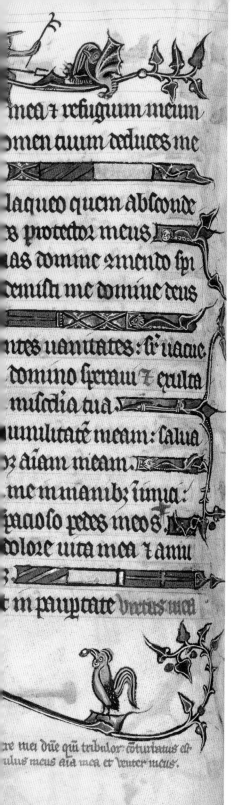

CONTENTS

INTRODUCTION

MORE MANUSCRIPTS survive from the Middle Ages than any other movable artefacts. Original manuscripts can be seen in public and university libraries, in cathedrals and museums, and in private collections and bookshops. One can still turn the pages of medieval manuscripts, admiring the handwritten script and feeling the slightly furry texture of the parchment pages. One can look at the decoration, watching the light sparkling off the burnished gold and noticing animals and birds half-hidden in the formal tangle of leaves and flowers. One can gaze at pictures and look straight into the eyes of an evangelist painted twelve hundred years ago or at fairytale Gothic landscapes of the fifteenth century. One can close the book, and feel its weight, and examine the medieval wooden binding. Then, if you have found a patient curator or rare books librarian, ask for another manuscript, and another, and start to notice the differences in the books brought out. Some will be vast and may need to be trundled out on a trolley, some will be small enough to fit into the palm of the hand, some will be written on what seems to be paper (it is, in fact, exactly that), and some will seem disappointing because they appear to have almost no decoration at all.

The three questions asked by those being shown medieval manuscripts for the first time will usually be: is it true that all these books were made by monks? How long did such marvels take to make? How was this done? (A fourth question, which we will ignore for the moment, is sometimes: what are they worth?)

Saint Jerome in his study, with his library kept in a curtained cupboard. (MS. Auct. D. inf. 2. 13, fol. 209v, Netherlands for the English market, third quarter of the fifteenth century)

9

It is impossible to approach questions about making manuscripts without understanding clearly from the outset that medieval manuscripts were being produced at all times during a period of about fifteen hundred years, between the late Roman Empire and the high Renaissance, in every part of Europe and in conditions as varied as it is possible to imagine, from hermits' cells in the mountains to sophisticated commercial production lines in the big cities. No specific statement about the production of a medieval manuscript can be applied to every example: the field is simply too vast to let us generalise. Nor is it easy to know where to begin or end the investigation. Every proposition raises another question about where or why some particular feature began or how it came to be there. Every conclusion is incomplete without asking what happened next.

In a little book like this covering such a long period, we cannot discuss style at all. The histories of handwriting and of pictorial art are extraordinarily interesting, as one stream mingles with another and branches off again in infinitely complex relationships. Each scribe or illuminator will write or paint in the manner of his time. One simply cannot go further than this without losing all thread of the narrative. Nor, in the end, can we necessarily answer many questions about the techniques used by the craftsmen. Any statements must be based on what one can see by scrutinising surviving illuminated manuscripts themselves, by sifting historical records, by studying written instructions of contemporary craftsmen, and sometimes by practical experiment in trying to recreate the process. It is a delicate balance. Sometimes there are no answers at all.

But let us take those three principal questions in order. Is it true that all these books were made by monks? The short answer is no. The long answer is less dogmatic. As Christianity advanced across

The evangelist Mark in a manuscript of the Greek New Testament. He is writing with, apparently, a reed pen. On a cupboard in front of him are the various tools and materials of a medieval scribe. (MS. Auct. T. inf. 1. 10, fol. 118v, eastern Mediterranean, second quarter of the twelfth century)

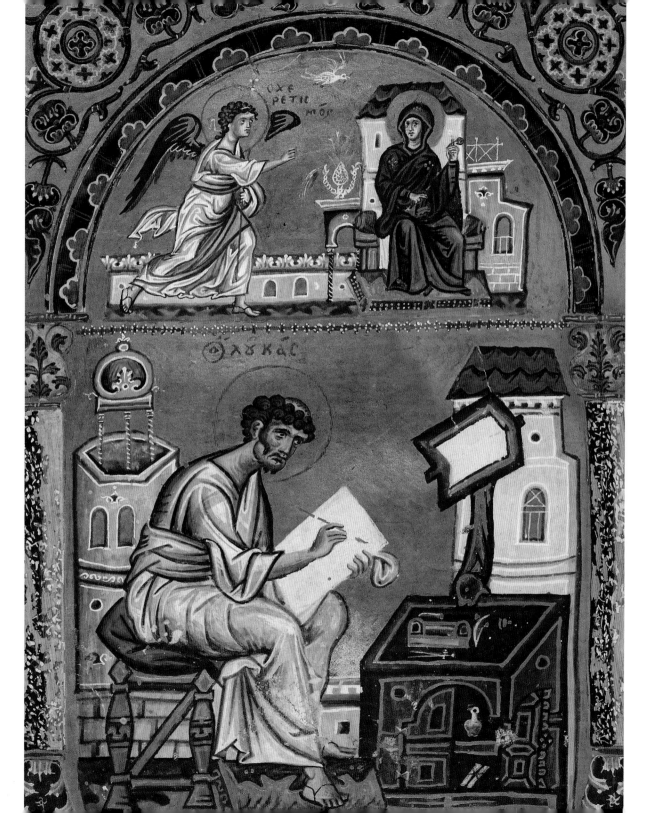

pagan Europe in the Dark Ages, it brought with it the Mediterranean skills of literacy and writing. The Rule of Saint Benedict encouraged monks and nuns in the use of books, and monasteries and religious communities needed libraries. Teaching children to read was one of the parochial duties of the Church, and perhaps most literate people in the Middle Ages had received some or all of their education from clerics. Until the eleventh or twelfth century, probably most manuscripts were indeed made in monasteries or churches. Monks sat in the cloisters copying and studying texts, and they devoted leisure and skill to doing so. There was not much private ownership of books a thousand years ago, and most religious communities simply produced manuscripts for their own use and for that of their dependents. Only a finite number of texts had ever been written, and theoretically a monastery could hope to be fairly comprehensive in its collection of several hundred manuscripts.

By about 1100, however, the number of new texts was increasing and monastic libraries found it more and more difficult to keep their collections up to date. Every passing decade added to the number of texts required. Monasteries began employing secular scribes and illuminators to collaborate in book production. By the end of the century early universities in Paris and Bologna had introduced an education which was more or less independent of the monasteries. There evolved a market for books owned by people of the secular world, whether students seeking textbooks or noble men and women commissioning Psalters for their private use. By around 1200 there is quite good evidence of secular workshops writing and decorating manuscripts for sale to the laity. In the mid-thirteenth century there were certainly bookshops in the big university and commercial towns, arranging the writing out of new manuscripts and trading in second-hand copies. By 1300 it must already have been exceptional for any monastery to make its own

manuscripts: usually, monks bought their books from shops like anyone else, although this is not quite true of the Carthusians or of some religious communities in the Netherlands.

If a layman in the fifteenth century wanted to buy a Book of Hours, for example, he would go to a bookshop or stationer and would commission one. Such shops were often clustered around the cathedrals and market squares of big towns. The customer might be shown second-hand copies for sale but if he wanted a new manuscript he would need to agree in advance the size and content

The oldest surviving manuscript of the Rule of Saint Benedict, written in uncial script and ornamented with simple decoration. (MS. Hatton 48, fols. 14v–15r, England (probably Canterbury), late seventh or early eighth century)

ugium pellium ugurca. Cale ii cozonam initeia
q̃ rp̃o beatorum aploz choz. talem retributionẽ re
cipiunt p̃ corruptabilibus.

and the extent of decoration, and doubtless the price. A deposit might be paid in advance. The various craftsmen would then be subcontracted. Sometimes the scribes seem to have lived with the stationers, or at least to have been employed on the premises, but illuminators, working at home among their families and apprentices, are often recorded in cheaper areas of town. They were all paid craftsmen, like any others, and often members of guilds. They were by no means anonymous monks and we know the names

Memoire de saint george. ã.

eorgi martir indite te decet laus
et gloria pre totatum militia y que

Prologue

Loenge a dieu soit au comencement
e tous mes dis · et aprez ensement
la treshaulte et noble fleur eslite
e les soues ou maint bon se delite
e puis a tous excellent prince et sauche

and addresses of very many late medieval scribes and illuminators.

Thus, to summarise so far, until about 1100 most books were indeed made by monks, and after about 1200 most were probably being produced independently of monasteries. The actual techniques used to make the books were not necessarily any different whether executed in a rural cloister or an urban attic studio. In the chapters which follow, some distinctions are made between the monastic age — which is generally earlier — and the secular period of the later Middle Ages. It is not a neat separation, and the dividing line is not always clear.

The second question, then, is how long manuscripts took to make. It depended on the length of the book, and who was making it. A monk had other commitments as well as book production, and not only attended chapel up to eight times a day but also took turns in duties around the monastery's school, kitchen, guest house or garden. There is evidence of some monastic manuscript-making projects extending over years, and doubtless such undertakings were often very much part-time occupations. An eleventh-century monastic scribe, in no great haste, might achieve three or four moderate-sized books a year. A professional scribe, however, working for a commercial bookshop in the fifteenth century, was paid by the job and not by the hour. There are manuscripts in which the scribe announces at the end that the work was started and finished in a matter of days. The Renaissance scribe Giovanni Marco Cinico, who mostly worked in Naples between 1458 and 1498, boasted that he wrote full-length manuscripts in fifty-two or fifty-three hours, for instance, and he was nicknamed *Velox*, 'speedy'. Perhaps a Book of Hours might usually be written out within a week, and the miniatures might well be executed at the rate of two or three a day. A professional artisan who knows his job and repeats it throughout a lifetime can often work extremely fast.

Christine de Pisan writing in her study at a table draped in cloth, with other completed manuscripts bound in red. (MS. Bodl. 421, fol. 1r, northern France, second quarter of the fifteenth century)

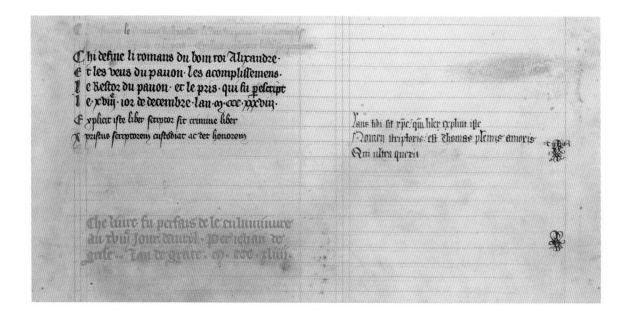

The chapters which follow make the process seem immensely slow as one stage is discussed after another. In practice, of course, many tasks took place simultaneously. The parchmenter is scraping last week's skins while this week's supply is soaking in vats in the shed. Fresh quills are drying out while the scribe is writing with earlier stock. The illuminator during a lunch break checks on the infusions of next week's pigments in the pantry. Certain devices for speeding the process further were evolved during the centuries, culminating at last in the invention of printing around 1450. The really very considerable production of medieval manuscripts in the centuries until then is the best possible evidence of a prolific and successful craft.

The third question, then, is how did they make them? Subject to all the caution noted above, read on.

Illumination might be supplied some time later than the text. The scribe here notes completion of a manuscript's text on 18 December 1338 and then, a few lines below, the artist records finishing the illumination on 18 April 1344. (MS. Bodl. 264, fol. 208r, Flanders, dated 1338–44)

The author presenting a lady with the completed and bound manuscript of his romance of the Earl of Toulouse. (MS. Ashmole 45, fol. 2r, England, early sixteenth century)

attelhere j parrochia sce marie de Oxonia. scilicet illa tota q iacet iter tram lamecti ligat
tram Emme ydexatcis i longitudine. y latitudine. tenenda y habenda illi y thdibz suis de
thdibz meis. i feodo y hyditate. libe. qete. plene. y integre. reddendo inde annuati in y thdibz
lle thdes suii iiij. solt. y oi sequtio. ad duos tminos i anno. scilicet ad natale dni duos solt.
j natiuitate sci Johis baptiste duos solt. Et ego helyas pdcs y thdes mei warantizabim pd
tram pdco Wille y thdibz suis cont omes homies mares y feminas q poterint mori y uiue. Et
hac cocessione. dimullione. y libatione. y warantizatione: pdict Willz dedit m i belsuma d
charecas arg. y uxori mee xviij. d. ad caldamta. Et q uolui ut omia pdca sic pdiuisa st fi
j stabilia pmaneat. hanc psente carta sigilli mei ipssione firmaui. His testibz. toraldo a
carlo. Alberno tornatore. Walto cori. Gidone textore. Alexandro fabro. Robto de northanti.
filio ei. pet illuminatore. Lado illuminatore. Witto illuminatore. Toma scptore. Reginaldo parcai
Roggo parcamei.

I. PAPER AND PARCHMENT

PARCHMENT is made from the skin of an animal. The process of transforming the animal skin into a clean white material suitable for writing medieval manuscripts was the task of the *percamenarius*, the 'parchment-maker' or parchmenter. Such professionals existed throughout the Gothic period and probably back into the Romanesque and Carolingian ages. Thus, in the year 822, Abbot Adelard instituted a parchment-maker among the officers of his abbey of Corbie in northern France, and there was a lay *percamenarius* in Regensburg in the early twelfth century. The earliest documentary evidence of book production in Oxford is a land charter dating from some time around 1215, witnessed by a scribe, three illuminators and two parchmenters whose names are Reginald and Roger. In thirteenth-century Florence, parchmenters had a shop beside the Badia. In Ghent in 1280 there were town statutes mentioning parchmenters. The Paris tax rolls of 1292 include names of nineteen parchmenters and the list is not complete. In the late Middle Ages parchmenters took their place among the artisans and tradesmen of every town.

In normal usage, the terms 'parchment' and 'vellum' are interchangeable. 'That stouffe that we wrytte upon: and is made of beestis skynnes: is somtyme called parchment somtyme velem', wrote William Horman in the early sixteenth century. In the manuscripts department of the Bodleian Library in Oxford the house usage today is to refer to the material consistently as parchment; in the British Library in London, the same substance

One of the earliest documents attesting to literary activity around Catte Street in Oxford is a land conveyance witnessed by a scribe, several illuminators and two parchmenters (Oxford University Archives WPβ/F/46, Oxford, early thirteenth century)

Apes preparing and scraping parchment, a satirical drawing in the lower margin of a romance of Alexander. (MS. Bodl. 264, fol. 84r, Flanders, completed in 1344)

is standardly called vellum. The material is the same. The word parchment, usually *pergamenum* in medieval Latin, derives from the name of the city of Pergamum whose ancient King Eumenes II is said by Pliny to have invented it in the second century BC during a trade blockade on papyrus. Recent extractions of DNA from manuscript pages are showing how seemingly identical skins within single manuscripts are sometimes made from different species of animal. The word vellum has the same origin as veal or *veau* in French, in other words, calf, *vitellus* in Latin, and is strictly the writing material made from the skin of young calves or small bullocks. (Fully grown cattle have skin too thick for use.) Doubtless most medieval scribes and readers of manuscripts neither knew nor cared what the animal had been when alive. 'Is not parchment made of sheepskins?', asks Hamlet in the graveyard; 'Ay, my lord', Horatio replies, 'and of calf-skins too' (5.1.111–12). Local convenience

A cow with her calf, from the Ashmole Bestiary. Calf-skin, especially that of new-born animals, provided some of the finest parchment of the Middle Ages. (MS. Ashmole 1511, fol. 30v, eastern England, early thirteenth century)

was probably a determining factor: sheep and goat around the Mediterranean, for example, but mostly cattle in Northumbria.

The preparation of parchment is a slow and complicated process. It will take some detail (as indeed it does in medieval recipes) to describe the stages of its manufacture. Early craftsmen's manuals emphasise that the selection of good skins is crucial. More so than in today's scientifically controlled agriculture, medieval farm animals probably suffered from diseases and ticks, and these can leave unacceptable flaws on the skin of the flayed animal. A parchmenter, looking over available skins in the abattoir, would probably also have to consider the colour of the wool or hair as this will be reflected on the final surface of the parchment: white sheep or calves will tend to produce white parchment, and the shadowy brown patterns, which are one of the aesthetically pleasing features of parchment, may often be echoes of a brindled calf or piebald goat.

First of all the parchmenter has to wash a skin in cold clear running water for a day and a night (according to one recipe) or simply 'til hit be clene ynoughe', according to another. As a skin begins to rot, the hair naturally falls out. In hot countries the damp skins may have been laid out in the sun to allow this action to take place. Usually, however, the process of loosening the hair in parchment-making is artificially induced by soaking the skins in wooden or stone vats in a solution of lime and water for between about three to ten days (longer in winter, apparently, and better too long than too short), stirring the vats several times a day with a wooden pole.

One by one, the wet slippery skins are scooped out and draped hairside out over a great curved upright shield of wood, called a beam. The parchment-maker stands behind the beam, leaning forward over the top, and scrapes the hair off with a long curved knife with a wooden handle at each end. The hair falls away surprisingly fast, slipping down into a soggy pile on the ground. The bare skin is revealed underneath, looking pink where the animal's hair was white and paler where it was brown. Where possible the outer film is scraped away too. This surface where the hair has been is known as the grain side of the parchment. The skin is still very wet and dripping with the lime solution. It may sometimes be re-immersed in the vat after the hair has been peeled away. In either case it is then flipped over on the wooden beam so that the original inner side is now outermost and the parchmenter once again leans over the board with the curved knife and pares away the residue of clinging flesh. If pushed too hard the knife can cut through the skin by mistake, and this energetic fast scraping requires a surprising delicacy of touch and experience. The de-haired and tidied-up pelt

A modern parchment-maker scraping hair off a wet, limed pelt draped over a parchmenter's beam.

is then once more rinsed for two further days in fresh water to clear it of the lime. This completes the first and smelliest stage of parchment-making.

In the second phase of the process the skin is actually made into parchment. It centres around the drying of the skin while it is stretched taut on a frame. The pelt, floppy and wet from its last rinse, is suspended spreadeagled in a wooden frame. This frame can be hoop-shaped (medieval instructions describe it as *circulus*) or more or less rectangular like the frame of a blackboard and about as big, as shown in a twelfth-century manuscript from Bamberg. The skin cannot be nailed to the frame because as it dries it shrinks and the edges would tear away (and in any case the frames are used over and over again and would become unserviceable if riddled with nail holes) and so instead the parchmenter suspends the skin by little strings attached to adjustable pegs in the frame. Every few centimetres around the edge of the skin the parchment-maker pushes little pebbles or compressed balls of waste parchment into the soft border, folding them in to form knobs which are then looped around and secured with cord. The other end of the cord is then anchored into the slot of a revolving peg in the frame. One by one these knobs and strings are lashed around the edge until the whole skin resembles a vertical trampoline, and the pegs are turned to pull the skin taut. As it stretches so any tiny gashes or cuts accidentally made in the flaying or de-hairing will be pulled out into circular or oval holes. It is not uncommon to see such holes in pages or margins of medieval manuscripts. If the parchmenter notices cuts in time they can be stitched up with thread to stop their expansion into holes; sometimes pages of manuscripts show holes with stitch marks around their edges, evidently indicating that cuts were mended but split their stitches and opened up again under pressure.

A drawing of a monk scraping parchment attached to a rectangular frame. (Bamberg, Staatsbibliothek, Cod. Patr. 5, fol. 1v, south Germany, twelfth century)

Mais as espees les tiumrat esleger. 201.

As port despaigne en e passet roll.

Sur ueillantif sun bon cheual curant.

Portet ses armes mult li sunt auenant.

Mais sun espiet uait li bers palmeiant.

Cuntre le ciel uait la mure turnant.

Laciet en su un gunfanun tut blanc.

Les renges li batent iosquas mains.

Cors ad mult gent le uis cler e riant.

Sun cupaignun apref le uait siuant.

7 cil de france le clement a guarant.

Vers sarrazins reguardet fierement.

E uers francs humeles 7 dulcement.

Si lur ad dit un mot curteisement. alez

Seignurs baruns suef pas tenant.

Cist paien uont grant martirie querant.

Encor aūrū un escher bel egent.

Kulf reis de france nout unkes si uaillant.

A cez paroles uint les oz a instant. Aor

Dist oliuer nai cure de parler.

Vostre olifan ne deignastes suner.

Ke de carlun mie uos nenauez.

Il nen set mot mad culpes li bers.

Cil ki la sunt ne sunt mie a blasmer.

Kar cheualchez a quanque uos puez.

Seignors baruns el camp uos retenez.

Pur deu uos pri ben seiez purpensez.

De colps ferir de receuir e de duner.

Cuts or flaws in skin can open up into oblong holes in parchment when it is stretched tightly during preparation, as here in the manuscript of the *Chanson de Roland*; the parchment-maker could sometimes catch the cuts in time and quickly sew them up. (MS. Digby 23, fols. 36v, 21v, England (possibly Oxford), twelfth century)

The skin is now tight and rubbery but still wet. The parchment-maker keeps it wet initially by ladling on scoops of hot water which run down the skin and puddle onto the ground. He then stands firmly, perhaps with one leg securely through the edge of the wooden frame, and begins scraping vigorously at the skin using a curved knife with a central handle. An ordinary knife would have a sharp corner and so could too easily cut the tight surface. The crescent-shaped knife was called a *lunellum* and occurs in medieval pictures of parchment-makers as their most recognisable tool, and is used to give both surfaces a really thorough scraping, especially over the flesh side of the skin. As the work progresses the parchmenter is constantly tightening the pegs and tapping them with a hammer to keep them fixed. Then the taut skin is allowed to dry on the frame, perhaps helped by exposing it to the sun as this stage is most effective if it happens fast, and it shrinks and becomes tighter still as it does so.

Scraped skins stretched on frames, laid out to dry under tension in a modern parchment-maker's workshop.

When it is all dry, the scraping and shaving begins again. The skin is now as taut as a new drum and the noise in the workshop of the metal knife on the surface is considerable. Fluffy little peelings fall away as layer after layer are pared off. Probably in the Middle Ages these shavings were swept up and saved to use later for boiling up to make glue. The amount of scraping will depend on the fineness of the parchment being made. In the early monastic period of manuscript production parchment was often quite thick, but by the thirteenth century it was being planed away to an almost tissue thinness. The grain side where the hair had once been has to be scraped away especially at this final stage to remove the glassy shine which is unsatisfactory as a writing surface.

Now the pegs can be undone. The dry thin opaque parchment is released and can be rolled up and stored or taken to be sold. Probably when medieval scribes or booksellers bought vellum from a *percamenarius* it was like this, not yet buffed up and rubbed with chalk in preparation for the actual writing. Prices of parchment of course varied greatly, but sheets were mostly sold by the dozen. The accounts of the Sainte-Chapelle in Paris include the expenses in 1298 of the huge quantity of 972 dozen skins at the cost of 194 *livres* and 18 *sous* (this works out at 3 *sous* a skin, a considerable sum), plus 24 *livres* and 6 *sous* for scraping them, and 60 *sous* to one Harvey for selecting the skins (that is, a half per cent) and 10 *sous* to the valuer. There are English references to parchment-makers charging 1¼d. per skin in 1301, 8s.8d. for six dozen leaves in 1312–13, 6s. for two dozen leaves in 1358–9 (both the latter can be divided out to just 3d. a sheet), but as much as £4.6s.8d. for the thirteen dozen skins of best calf (*percamenti vitulini*) for the luxurious Litlyngton Missal for Westminster Abbey in 1383–4. This then cost just over 6½ d. a sheet, and was the second largest expense after the gold in making the

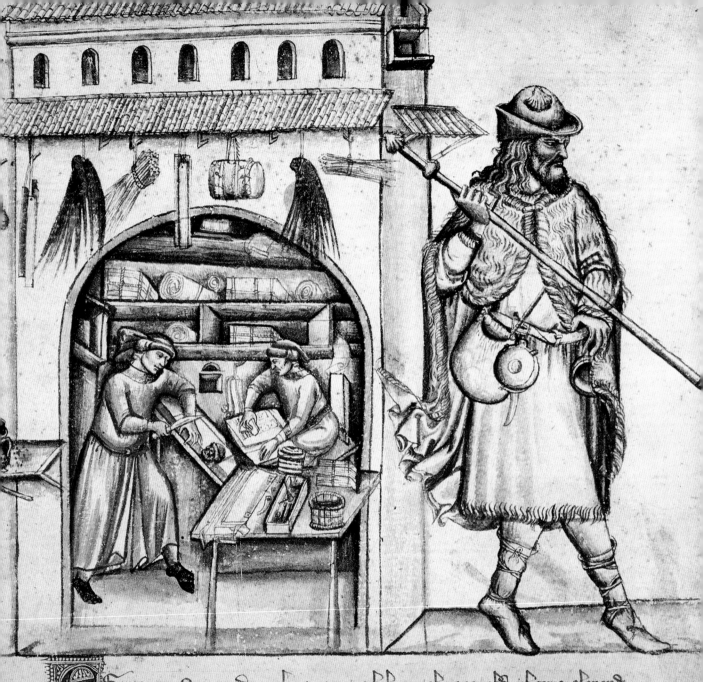

Sonto un peregrin de molte parte / che l'anno e l'mexe e d'i e come e quand
de le chose chen stade / e ver qual pando, et olle adun racolte cheran sparte.
Onde chi vol deletto deste carte / sil togla / eno le moua de qui stando
che se s lo fesse si chadmie in bando / de quel che tutto per raxon comparte.

Perche le piedro sta sempre mie hosto / eda s a deregistrar chaxone

book. It was evidently top-quality parchment for a book intended
to be a monument forever.

Parchment is extraordinarily durable, far more so than
leather, for instance. It can last for a thousand years, or more,
in perfect condition. Good parchment is soft and thin and velvety,
and folds easily. It can be fascinating to turn a few pages of a
medieval manuscript peering through a magnifying glass at the
surface. No facsimile can ever replicate the tactile and even sensual
experience of handling and running one's fingers across soft leaves
of medieval parchment. Even the smell is quite different from
that of paper, and in fact varies enormously with manuscripts from
one country to another. Within moderation, a bit of handling is
said to be good for manuscripts because parchment, like leather,
responds well to movement and can lose suppleness if untouched
for centuries.

The grain side of the sheet, where the hair once was, is usually
darker in colour, creamy or yellower (especially with sheep
parchment) or brownish grey with goat parchment. The grain side,
too, tends to curl in on itself. In some poorer quality scholastic
manuscripts, made of cheap parchment, this curling tendency is so
marked that the pages can almost roll up before one's eyes. This is
because when it was on the animal the outer side was less elastic
and, after being released from the tension of the parchmenter's
frame, it tends to contract rather more than the original flesh side.
The better the vellum, the more suede-like the grain surface feels
because its outer layer has had to be pared right away and we are
experiencing the furry inside texture of the skin. Especially in
Italian manuscripts, the ink tends not to adhere so well to this side
and it looks a dusty brown. Through a magnifying glass one can
sometimes (not always) see constellations of tiny dots which were
once hair follicles.

The shop of a medieval parchment-seller, showing sheets being trimmed and rubbed with chalk, and a selection of rolls and packets of ready-folded parchment for sale. (Bologna, Biblioteca universitaria, MS. 1456, fol. 4r, Italy, fifteenth century)

Turn the skin over to the flesh side and it is noticeably whiter than the grain side and usually smoother and it tends to be convex, naturally curling away. If one is permitted to fan out the edges of half a dozen or so adjacent pages of a medieval parchment manuscript, this difference of colour becomes very striking: yellow/white/yellow/white/yellow and so on. The implications of this will be considered in a moment when we come to the process of folding the parchment sheets into book format. Sometimes too one can see tree-like vein marks on parchment, the result of blood in the skin when the animal died (this ought to be more common in pelts from hunted animals, like deer, or those that died naturally in the field, than from those killed and bled quickly in a butcher's shop, but it is difficult to know how to set about proving it). If the flaws were too rough and pronounced and yet the scribe decided to use the sheet nonetheless, a ring may have been drawn around the blemish and the scribe's subsequent writing parts like the Red Sea to flow around it. On big pages one can sometimes detect denser ridges, like the contour marks of a mountain range shown on a relief map, where the backbone transected the skin, and perhaps on one edge one may observe (aided perhaps by imagination) the scalloped curve which was the neck of the animal.

There is a vexed and unresolved question of uterine vellum. Old-fashioned texts about medieval manuscripts assert that the finest medieval parchment was made from the skin of aborted calves, and the term is still sometimes used to describe that extremely thin silky parchment used to perfection in tiny thirteenth-century Paris Bibles. There is some medieval evidence that aborted skin was valuable and desirable, and it is true that parchment made from this rather unappealing material or from the skins of very newly born animals does indeed look and feel like that which antiquarians call uterine vellum. However, it is very difficult to

Consecutive leaves of a disbound glossed Gospel of Matthew show the difference in colour between alternate hair and flesh sides of the folded parchment. (MS. Laud Misc. 439, probably England, first half of the thirteenth century)

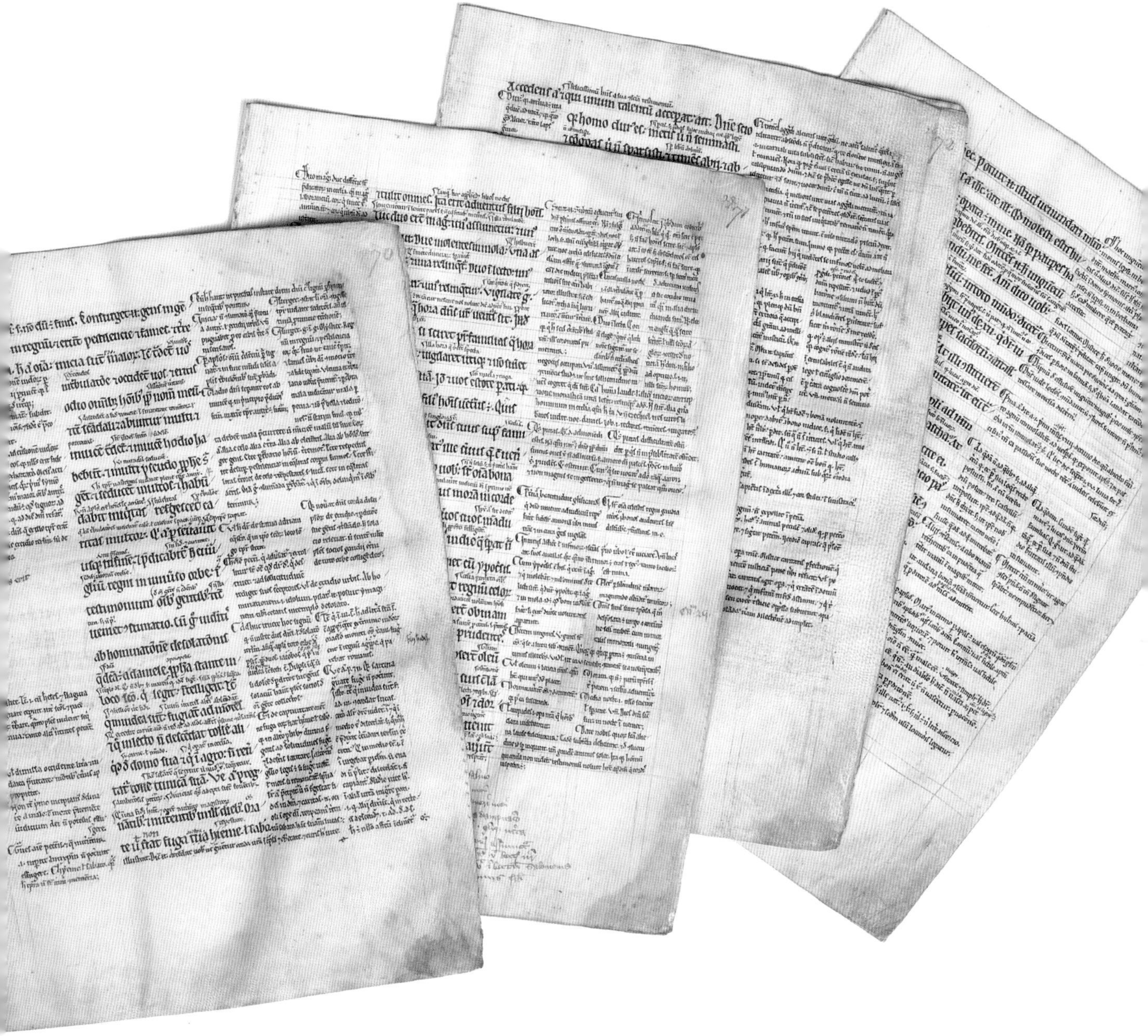

believe that thousands of cows miscarried for generations, or were deprived of their foetuses in such numbers to supply the booktrade economically. It may simply be a result of paring calf skin down and down so that only the tissue-thin membrane remained, or perhaps the skins were sometimes split to produce two sheets out of a single thickness. Again there is some (not much) medieval evidence for this taking place. If the term uterine parchment must be used at all, it should perhaps refer to a quality of skin and not to its origin.

This lengthy discussion of the parchment-maker's work ought to be tempered with a reminder that not all medieval manuscripts were written on parchment. The Middle Ages opened with a long legacy of papyrus book production, and this fragile Egyptian reed material lingered on in occasional use until the seventh or even eighth century. Papyrus is inexpensive to make and suitable for writing scrolls but is not satisfactory for texts bound in book form because pages tend to snap off when they are turned repeatedly and the folds are not strong enough to support constant pressure on sewing threads in the centre of the gatherings. The word *papyrus*, however, survives in modern English in our word 'paper'. There are indeed very many medieval manuscripts written on paper. Cheap little books made for clerics and students were probably more often on paper than on parchment by the fifteenth century. Even major aristocratic libraries did not despise manuscripts on paper. The inventory of the library of the dukes of Burgundy in about 1467 lists just over nine hundred volumes, recording usually whether the books were written on parchment or on paper; 196 manuscripts, just over 20 per cent of the total in the most princely library in northern Europe, were described as written on paper. Two volumes in the ducal collection are described as mixed paper and parchment, 'moictié papier, moictié parchemin'. Some paper manuscripts survive like this with the inner and outer pairs of leaves in each gathering made of

Manuscripts in classical times had been written either as papyrus scrolls or as *codices*, in the format of modern books, both shown here in the *Noticia dignitatum*, illustrating the responsibilities of a Roman curator of libraries. (MS. Canon. Misc. 378, fol. 146v, Italy (probably Padua), dated 1436)

FL. INTAILL COMORD PR.
FL. VALE MAG EP. IVSS dd
FL. INTAILL COMORD PR.
FL. VALE MAG EPIS. IVSS dd.
FL. INTAILL COMORDI PR.
FL VALE MAG EPIS IVSS. dd

Magister memorie annotationes oms dictat & emittit. respond
tamen et precibus

The double sorwe of Troilus to tellen
That was the k"ing Priamus sone of Troye
In lovinge how his auntures befellen
from wo to wele, and afer out of Joye
My prpos is, or that I parte ʒow fro
Thesiphone thow help me for tendyte
Thise wofull vers that wepinth as I wryte

To the clepe I thow goddesse of torment
Thow cruell furie sorwinge euer in peyne
Help me þ am the sorowfull instrument
that helpith loueres as I can complayne
For wele sitt yt the sothe for to seyne
A wofull wight to haue a drery fere
And to a sorowfull tale a sory chere

For I that god of Loues seruantes serue
Ne darr to loue for myn vnliklynesse
Preyen for spede, all sholde I therfor sterue
So fer am I fram his help in derknesse
But nathelees if this may doon gladnesse
Vnto any loue, and his cause auaille
Haue he my thank, and myn be this trauaille

But ʒe loueres that bathen in gladnesse
Iff any drope of pitee in ʒow be
Remembreth ʒow on passed heuynesse
That ʒe haue felt, and on the aduersite
Off other folk, and thinketh how þ ʒe
Haue felt þ loue durst ʒow displese
Or ʒe haue wonne hym wt to grete an ese

And preyeth for theme þ ben in the cas
Off Troilus, as ʒe may after here
That loue theme bringe in heuene to solas
And eke for me preyeth to god so dere
That I haue myʒt to shewe in sum manere
Swich peyne and wo as Loues folk endure

parchment, presumably because parchment is (or was assumed to be) stronger and these were the most vulnerable pages.

Paper was a Chinese invention probably of the second century and the technique of papermaking spent a thousand years slowly working its way through the Arab world to the West. By the thirteenth century there were established paper mills in Spain and Italy, and in France by about 1340, Germany by 1390, but probably not in England until the later fifteenth century. Paper was exported from its place of manufacture into all parts of Europe and the first paper manuscripts were administrative records, merchants' accounts, and other more or less ephemeral texts. By about 1400 it was becoming a relatively common medium for little volumes of sermons, inexpensive textbooks, popular tracts and so on. As late as 1480 a ruling of the University of Cambridge stipulated that only books on parchment could be accepted as security for loans. Paper was evidently thought to be too insignificant. It was the invention of printing in the 1450s which transformed the need for paper, and by the later fifteenth century it had become so infinitely cheaper than parchment that it was being used for all but the most luxurious books, as it still is today.

Medieval paper was made from linen rags. It is much stronger and more durable than modern wood-pulp paper, and fifteenth-century scribes were wrong if they believed that it would not survive. Very briefly, rag paper is manufactured as follows. White rags are sorted and washed thoroughly in a tub pierced with drainage holes and they are then allowed to ferment for four or five days. Then the wet disintegrating pieces are cut into scraps and beaten for some hours in clean running water, left to fester for a week, beaten again, and so on, several times over, until the mixture disintegrates into a runny waterlogged pulp. It is then tipped into a huge vat. A wire frame is scooped into the vat, picking

By the late Middle Ages even quite grand literary manuscripts were written on paper, such this copy of Chaucer's *Troilus and Criseyde* written in Scotland for the Sinclair family. (MS. Arch. Selden B. 24, fol. 1r, Scotland, after 1488)

up a film of wet fibres, and it is shaken free of drips and emptied onto a sheet of felt. Another layer of felt is laid over it. As the soggy sheets emerge and are tipped out, they are stacked in a pile of multiple sandwiches of interleaved felt and paper. Then the stack is squeezed in a press to remove excess water and the damp paper can be taken out and hung up to dry. When ready, the sheet is 'sized' by lowering it into a glue made from boiling scraps of parchment or other animal offcuts. The size makes the paper less absorbent and allows it to take ink without running. The sheets may have to be pressed again to make them completely flat. Sometimes, especially in north-east Italy (doubtless under the influence of Islamic paper manufacture), the paper was polished with a smooth stone to give it a luxurious sheen.

It happens of course that the wire frame leaves lines where the soft paper pulp is thinner, and by at least 1300 European paper-makers began twisting little patterns out of wire and attaching them to the grid so that amusing or emblematic pictures were coincidentally transferred into the thickness of the paper, invisible when the paper was stacked or folded in a book but quite clear when held up to the light. Thus watermarks came into being as a means of distinguishing paper stocks and their makers. Watermarks are one of the most common and most self-effacing classes of medieval pictorial art, but they lie hidden waiting to be detected in the thickness of pages of second-class manuscripts: whole bestiaries of lions, bears, boars, basilisks, unicorns, eagles, swans, lobsters, elephants (two instances have been recorded of elephants, in Italian paper used in Brussels in 1366 and Perpignan in 1380), sheep, oxen, horses, hounds, deer, fish, paschal lambs, angels, suns, stars, moons, mountains, castles, shields, helmets, swords, bows and arrows, axes, crowns, orbs, flags, cardinals' hats, ships, anchors, bellows, scissors, keys, bells, pairs of spectacles (first recorded in an

Watermarks in the thickness of paper can conceal multiple designs, like this gothic letter 'y' in a manuscript of Chaucer, revealed by beta-radiograph photography. (MS. Arch. Selden B. 24, fol. 32[r], Scotland, after 1488)

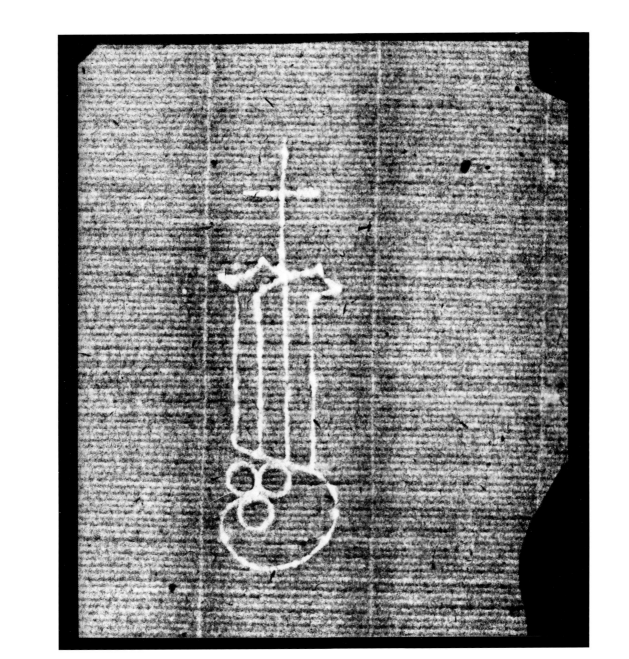

Italian watermark used in Bourges in 1387), flowers, hunting horns
and so forth, thousands of images full of delight and elusiveness.

Before a late medieval scribe could begin to write out a
manuscript, a decision had to be made whether to use paper or
parchment. Paper was cheaper and lighter and had the advantage of
being supplied in sheets of an exact format. Parchment was thought
to be stronger and has a slightly springy writing surface which
gives an agreeable flexibility to penstrokes as compared with the
unyielding flatness of writing on paper. (As a modern parallel, it is
easier and more tempting to write calligraphically with a soft felt-tip
pen than with a metal-ended ballpoint.) The most beautiful and
luxurious manuscripts were always on parchment, which was used
for Books of Hours and other traditional books intended for a
long life.

Parchment or paper as finished by the parchmenter or paper-
maker was supplied in large rectangular sheets. Dimensions of a
parchment skin are determined by the shape of the original animal
and, as animals are oblong (with legs at each end), so the sheets
similarly emerge oblong even when their irregular edges have been
squared off. (We shall return to this observation later.) A book is
not made up of single pages, but of pairs of leaves or bifolia. Several
pairs of leaves are assembled one inside another, folded vertically
down the middle and they can be stitched through the central
fold to make a book in its simplest form. The very earliest Coptic
manuscripts in 'codex' form (that is, with turning pages rather than
in continuous scroll format) were often constructed of a single
huge stack of bifolia folded right in the centre of the book, like a fat
American Sunday newspaper. The unwieldiness of this led scribes
in the early centuries of Christianity to begin assembling their
manuscripts out of a whole series of smaller gatherings sewn one
beside another. Modern hard-bound books are still made in exactly

the same way. Each clutch of folded bifolia is called a gathering or quire or signature. All standard medieval manuscripts are made up of gatherings. This is absolutely crucial. It is probably the single most important observation that can be made about the making of medieval books. A manuscript is a unit formed by assembling in sequence a series of smaller units. Scribes and illuminators worked on a gathering at a time. If one is examining a medieval manuscript carefully today, the first task will often be to peer into the centre of the folded pages looking for the sewing threads and sketching out a physical plan of where each gathering begins and ends. One may then begin to notice changes of scribe and illuminator, dividing their labour according to the gatherings.

A gathering is usually of eight leaves, or four bifolia. In early Irish manuscripts and in fifteenth-century Italian books a gathering might be of ten leaves. Little thirteenth-century Bibles, which used exceedingly thin parchment, were frequently formed of gatherings of twelve, sixteen, or even twenty-four leaves. Sometimes a book was made up mostly of gatherings of eight leaves but ended with a gathering of six or ten leaves because the conclusion of the text fitted more neatly. Even within a manuscript there may be gatherings of irregular length, and these can be clues as to how the maker put the book together. The Calendar of a liturgical manuscript, for instance, commonly has twelve leaves (for the twelve months) and will usually prove to be formed either of two gatherings of six leaves or one of twelve within a book otherwise uniformly in gatherings of eight leaves. In other words, the Calendar was made separately and could be extracted and changed without cutting into any other gatherings. This is a clue not only to the creation but also to the ongoing use of the manuscript.

A great deal of effort has been expended by historians of medieval books in trying to determine how the gatherings were

actually made. It is evidently not as simple as it sounds. Let us
remind ourselves that there are the subtle differences between
what had been the hair side and what had been the flesh side of
a sheet of parchment. In handmade paper too, if one can peer
closely enough, one can detect from which side the wire lines and
watermark were indented. Now open any medieval manuscript.
Almost without exception in over a thousand years of book
production in every conceivable circumstance all over Europe, facing
pages match. Hair side faces hair side, flesh side faces flesh side,
and in paper manuscripts watermark side faces watermark side. This
is quite extraordinarily consistent, and yet no medieval manuals
of craftsmanship mention the fact. A break in the sequence of hair
to hair, flesh to flesh, is so rare that it is often the first indication
that a leaf is missing from the manuscript. It would be pleasant to
suppose that scribes were merely hoping for a balanced effect of
double pages by matching up the very slight differences of texture
between the surfaces; this may be true, but it is too consistent,
occurring even in rough volumes where scribes evidently cared little
for appearance. The matching of surfaces was obviously so basic
that it must have come about without effort.

For what follows we are going to recommend that the reader
conducts a simple experiment while following this paragraph.
(This may be unorthodox, but it will be infinitely clearer than
complicated diagrams or apparently repetitive prose, and the
result will be dramatic.) Take an ordinary-shaped oblong sheet of
paper coloured or somehow marked on one side. Lay the paper
horizontally on the table with the colour side upwards. Now fold
it over once with a vertical crease in the middle. It looks tall and
thin. It is the shape called folio. Now fold it in half again and crease
it along the middle horizontally. It is oblong but a bit squatter in
shape. This format is called quarto, because four thicknesses are

folded. Now fold it in half yet again. The wad is now an eighth of the size that it began, and the shape is called octavo. Now stop. Imagine this as a gathering in a book, with a central fold and uncut edges like a French novel. Take a knife or a finger and open it up page by page as if you were reading it. Page 1 is white. Pages 2 and 3 facing each other are coloured. Pages 4 and 5 facing each other are white. Pages 6 and 7 are coloured, and so on. If this were vellum, in other words, no matter how many times you fold the sheet, flesh side will automatically face flesh side and hair side automatically face hair side. Presumably, then, this is more or less how gatherings were folded in the Middle Ages.

Now take another sheet. Place it horizontally before you also with the colour side upwards. Fold it over lengthways, making a long strip. Now imagine the strip divided into quarters along its length. Fold the first quarter over and crease it. Then fold both first and second quarters over again covering the third quarter, and crease it again. Finally fold the whole thing over on itself. You are left, as before, with a page-shaped package, an eighth of the size of the initial sheet. Imagine the last fold you have made as the centre of the gathering. Once again, slit it open. Again you will have a gathering of eight leaves with coloured and blank sides automatically facing each other.

In both these simple origami experiments we began with the test sheet colour side up. It makes a model with its first and last pages plain. If the sample had begun with the colour side downwards, the first and last pages would have come out coloured. In manuscripts from the late Roman Empire and from the Greek Orthodox world, the first and last pages of a gathering are the original flesh side. This was revived by the humanist manuscript-makers of fifteenth-century Italy. But for the rest of Europe from the pre-Carolingian to high Gothic periods, the first and last pages of a gathering are the original hair side of the parchment. It must simply be that the classical parchment folders began hair side up, and the medieval folders began flesh side up, and so fixed was the tradition that it seldom varied.

As one folds the sheet in half, in quarters, eighths, sixteenths and so on, it will always come out taller than it is wide. This is obvious, because the original sheet was rectangular, not square. Evidently parchment was folded to such a formula that when paper was introduced it too was manufactured in a similar rectangular format, and the folding produced the same effect. But the reason for the shape (to revert to the point of six paragraphs back) is because animals are oblong, and the reason why books even today are taller than they are wide is because in their medieval ancestry there was a millennium when they were made from folding animal-shaped parchment. This is not necessarily anything to do with size. Manuscripts can be absolutely vast, like the choirbooks of sixteenth-century Spain or the thirteenth-century Codex Gigas in Stockholm nearly a metre high, to little jewel-like prayerbooks half the size of a matchbox.

Evidently the simple folding of parchment is not the only explanation of constructing gatherings as it is difficult to see how ten-leaf units come about. (In an earlier edition of this book, I issued a challenge to readers to tell me how to fold paper to achieve this result: someone wrote from Auckland to suggest a solution but I regret that I have forgotten what it was.) The case is complicated further by the tantalising possibility that at least sometimes medieval scribes wrote their gatherings before they had been cut at all. This is an immensely worrying subject. Palaeographers have been driven to distraction arguing one way and the other, basing their generalisations on exceptionally rare fragments which have survived against all odds showing parts of texts written out on

An unfinished and entirely uncut sheet from a Book of Hours which must have been written before folding and cutting. (Paris, Bibliothèque nationale de France, MS. lat. 1107, fol. 400r, France, late fifteenth century)

te deus meternum. oro
eus qui xpi
sti sege mon
sum summitate mon
tis synay et in eodem so
co per sanctos angelos
tuos corpus beate kate
rine virginis et mris mi
rabiliter collocasti tri
bue nobis ut eius meritis
et intercessione ad mon
tem xpi... est... vale

entirely uncut sheets with eight pages on one side and eight on the other. The scribe needs to calculate the imposition (the page layout on the uncut sheet): p. 1 is in the second quarter of the lower half of the sheet, p. 2 is on its verso in the third quarter on the other side, p. 3 is next to it to the left, p. 4 is on its verso on the first side, p. 5 is upsidedown above p. 4, p. 6 is on its verso again, and so on, all worked out in advance so that when the sheet was eventually folded and cut open all sixteen pages ran on continuously from beginning to end. Durham Cathedral MS.A.IV.34 seems to have been made like this in the twelfth century, but it is surely exceptional. It seems unlikely to have been a practical method. There is, however, quite good evidence that sometimes gatherings were folded and cut open all except for a few millimetres of joined parchment which were left at the very top corner by the central fold. This allows the leaves to be opened and written page by page before the final snip which would separate them. If the leaves had already become separated, they could be held temporarily by a little twisted vellum ribbon nipped through the inner corner. A very few such fragile ephemeral thongs survive, but mostly they would be trimmed away when the edges were planed in binding. All these possibilities, however, must be regarded with caution. A few chance traces of tacking of gatherings are not necessarily indicative of universal practice.

In the earlier Middle Ages scribes probably assembled their gatherings and wrote in them as they worked through the transcription of a book. By the fifteenth century, at the latest, stationers were certainly selling paper and parchment already folded into gatherings. The inventory of stock of the deceased Florentine stationer and bookseller Giovanni di Michele Baldini in 1426, for example, included gatherings already made up for sale, such as twelve quires of parchment *da Salteri et Donadelli* (suitable for little Psalters and Donatus grammar books) and six quires *da messali* (for big Missals). Fifty years later the inventory of the stock of Gherardo e Monte di Giovanni in Florence included parchment for sale either by the skin or by the gathering and at most stages in between. We may be arguing in circles if we see this as proof that gatherings were pre-prepared. Scribes worked for stationers; for stationers to sell blank gatherings might simply indicate speculative preparation of more than their own needs.

This has been a long chapter so far and we have not yet approached the moment when the scribe began to write. There is still one further important preparatory stage. Lines were ruled on the pages of medieval manuscripts as a guide for the script. Schoolchildren today have lines ruled for their handwriting, and exercise-books and ledgers are printed with ruled lines. It is, however, considered now to be not really good manners to write formal letters on ruled paper, as if there were something a bit shameful in needing guide lines for handwriting. It was quite the reverse in the Middle Ages. The smarter the book, the more elaborately it was ruled. Unruled manuscripts (and they exist) are the cheap and ugly home-made transcripts. Splendidly illuminated manuscripts have grids of guide lines. When printing was introduced and early customers expected their books to resemble traditional manuscripts, the usual trick was to rule in guide lines around every line of printed text because writing presumably looked naked without it. There are examples of this at least into the seventeenth century. Ruled guide lines were an expected feature of a medieval book.

The lines drawn on a page of a medieval manuscript will depend very much on the text to be written. Either the scribe ruled his own, or he selected ruled leaves in accordance with the scale and page layout of his text. There is a ninth-century instruction for laying out

pastor eterne o clemēs
o bone custos qui dūi
denoti gregis preces
attenderes uoce supla

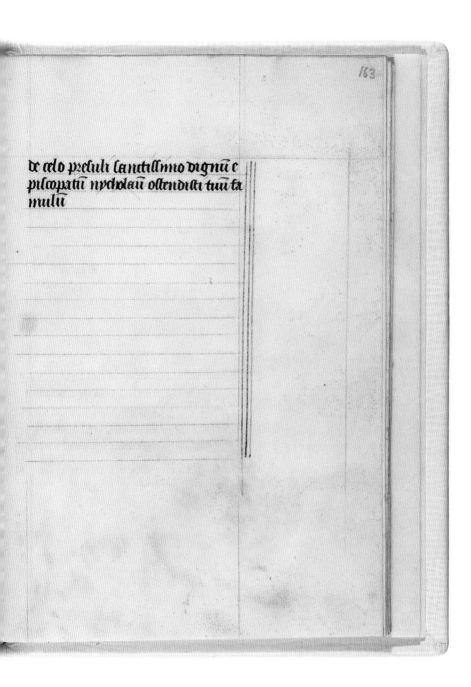

de celo preculi sanctissimo dignu e
piscopatu nycholau ostendisti tuu fa
multu

Pages were ruled before decisions had been made about the placement of pictures, as here in an unfinished Book of Hours. (MS. Douce 267, fols. 162v–163r, France (Besançon), second half of the fifteenth century)

Heore tale þei tolden. Wiþouten leo.
And on heore knees. gunne falle.
And seide. Sire þe kyng of Dayo
Of biffed Wordes. mo not scaye
Heyene Hound. he doþ ye calle
And ey his douȝter. he ȝine ye tille.
Wyn herte blod he Wol spille
And ȝe Baȝouns. Also
þon ye Soudan. þis I heyde
As a Wodman. he feyde.
His Robe. he rente adoun
He tay ye hey of hed. and Beþ
And seide he Wolde biline Wroþeþ
Weo his lord. seynt Mahoun.

þe Dable adoun riȝt he smot
In to ye floo. foot hot
He loked. as a Wylde lyon.
Al þat he hitte. he smot doun riȝt
Boþe seyȝaunt. and kniȝt
Erl. and eke Baȝoun.
Go he seyde. forsoye a pliȝt.
Al a day. and al a niȝt.
Þat no mon. miȝt hym chaste
A morwen Whon hit was day liȝt
He sente his messageys out riȝt
After his Baȝouns. in haste.

Lordynges he sey. What to gede
ay is don a gret misdede
Of Dayo. ye Cristene kyng
I bed him boȝe. lond and lede
To haue his douȝter. in Worþi bede
And spouse hye. Wiþ my þyng
And he seide. Wiþouten fayle
Liȝt he Wolde me sle. in Batayle
And mony a gret lordyng
He seyte he schal be for sþore
Or to Wroþehele. þat he was boȝe
Bote he hit þei to bryng.

Þerfore lordiȝes I haue afteros sent
ffor to come. to my pliment
To Wite. of ȝoub counsayle.
And alle onsþeyde. Wiþ good entent
ȝei Wolde be. at his comaundement
Wiþ outen eny fayle.

And Whon yei Were alle. at his heste
þe Soudan made. a Wel gret feste
ffor loue. of his Batayle.
þe Soudan gedeȝt. an ost vnyde
Wiþ Sarazins. of muchel pryde
þe kyng of Dayo. to assayle

Whon ye kyng hit heyde þat tyde
He seite aboute. on vche a syde
Alle þat he miȝte of sounde
Hieȝ Weye. ȝo bi gon to syake
ffor ye manaȝe. ne moste be-take
Of þat aȝayden heerde.

Batayle yei sette. vppon a day
Hit ȝine ye yȝrde day of may
No lengor. nolde yei lende
þe Soudan com. Wiþ gret polkey
Wiþ hosin baȝt. and fey þancey
Vppon þat kyng. to Wende

þe Soudan ladde. an huge ost
And com Wiþ muche pruine & Gost
Wiþ ye kyng of Dayo to fiȝte
Wiþ him. mony a Sarazin fey

pages mathematically. Suppose the page to be five units high and four wide, it says. The height of the written space should be four such units. The inner and lower margins should be three times as wide as the outer margin and as the gutter between the columns (if it is a two column book) and a third wider than the width of the upper margin. The lines should be spaced, the ninth-century directive concludes, according to the size of the writing. It is quite difficult to measure out a page according to these rules. Probably most manuscripts were simply arranged as elegantly as practicable without elaborate mathematics. It can be hard to confirm whether extant manuscripts followed a formula of proportion, because their three outer margins are likely to have been trimmed a number of times in rebinding over the centuries. If nothing else, however, medieval book designers probably realised that in a handsome manuscript the height of the written space equalled the width of the page.

The number of columns varies with the century and with the text. Very early codices often have several columns, presumably echoing their evolution from rolls, and primitive Irish books can be in one or two columns. Carolingian manuscripts and their Italian Renaissance imitations are usually in one wide column. Romanesque and Gothic textbooks are generally in two columns. French and German literary romances, with short lines, are frequently in three columns. Books of Hours are usually in one column, and Breviaries usually in two. Glossed biblical manuscripts are usually in three columns: a broadly spaced central column for the scriptural text and narrowly ruled outer panels for the commentaries in smaller script. Law texts often have a double column central block with three-sided compartments of gloss fitting to the left or the right around the main text. Some page layouts are so distinctive that one can identify a category of book at ten paces, without reading a word.

The Vernon manuscript of Middle English verse and prose is mostly written in three columns. (MS. Eng. poet. a. I, fol. 50v, England, late fourteenth century)

Until the twelfth century, most manuscripts were ruled in drypoint, that is, with blind lines scored into the parchment with a stylus or back of the knife. Scribes ruled hard and sometimes cut through the parchment by mistake. A benefit of scoring lines is that several pages could be impressed at once. A disadvantage is that if a scribe writes across a scored line the ink tends to run into the trough, and, on the other side of the sheet, there would be a ridge which can snag a quill pen and cause the ink to splatter. For this reason Carolingian scribes tend to write between the ruled lines, using them as the limits of ascenders and descenders, rather than actually on the base line, as Gothic scribes did and we do today. This has unstudied implications for understanding the shape of medieval scripts.

Around the late eleventh century we first find guide lines ruled in what looks like pencil: it could be graphite but is more likely to be metallic lead or even silver. Oblong pieces of lead have been excavated inscribed with names like ROGERII and KAROLI SCRIPTORIS in thirteenth- or fourteenth-century capitals, and are probably plummet markers for just such purposes as ruling manuscripts. From the thirteenth century onwards, concurrently with plummet (sometimes even in one manuscript), lines can be ruled in pen and ink. We find brown, red, green or purple ink used, and sometimes combinations of colours giving a festive appearance. Patient codicologists have tried to count up all the different possible patterns of ruling, recording literally hundreds of varieties but wresting very few conclusions from their statistics. Very often the lines marking off the block of text continue right to the edge of the page, and sometimes they are double or treble. The horizontal lines for the script sometimes extend to the edges too, or perhaps the first and last will, or the first, third, antepenultimate and last. It is interesting to look at a manuscript and notice how it has been ruled, but it is not easy to draw particular generalisations about what one sees.

Ruling page by page before even beginning to write was slow and tedious. Various devices were used to speed the process. The most universal was to measure out the first page of the gathering, or the outer or central pages together if the gathering was laid open, and to follow the lines with a rule to the extreme edge of the page and there to prick very hard right through the whole stack of leaves. Then all that was needed was to open the pages and join up the prickings and the ruling pattern would be duplicated exactly from page to page. Sometimes these holes were apparently pricked with the very tip of a knife because they are the shape of tiny triangular wedges. Commonly they must have been pushed with a carpenter's awl, a metal spike on a wooden handle.

Prickings are not always visible as they were frequently trimmed off in binding. If they occur in the inner margins as well as the outer margins, the leaves must have been ruled while the gatherings were folded into pages. Occasionally one notices (especially if alerted to look out for it) that every eight or ten lines or so one hole will be crooked or unduly widely spaced. If this is consistent in several gatherings, it is a good clue that the prickings had been made with some kind of wheel, like a tiny garden roller with spikes, and that one spike had somehow become knocked out of alignment and thus the defect recurred at regular intervals as the wheel went round. There is sometimes evidence too in the later Middle Ages that the multiple lines for the text were ruled with several pens tied together, like the *rastrum* or rake used for making musical staves. If for any reason these pens were knocked or quivered slightly as they were drawn across the page, the quaver is reflected at exactly the same point in several lines simultaneously. This is another clue worth looking out for in a page of manuscript.

A final artificial device, used only in the fifteenth century (as far as has been traced) and mostly in north-eastern Italy, is the ruling frame. This is a familiar feature of Oriental and Hebrew book production. Holes are drilled in a wooden board and wires are ingeniously threaded through, emerging in a criss-cross pattern exactly like that of the framework to be transferred onto the page. Then all that is needed is to place the blank sheet over the board and rub it with the fist, and the lines will be impressed identically onto the sheet. An inventory of a paper merchant in Perugia in 1463 includes *due tabule ad rigandum*, presumably two frames like this. Once more, as with other ruling devices, it is not necessarily easy to tell when confronting a manuscript if a ruling board has been used. But imagine how the wires must bisect each other on the board when they cross at right angles. One must be threaded under the other or pushed right through the wood and out again on the other side of the wire it crosses. One can see this in the manuscript, as no line actually crosses another; the lines stop fractionally short and pick up again a millimetre on the other side of the crossing. When a line is ruled with a stylus, it simply ploughs straight across, one way and the other.

In the early Middle Ages, scribes doubtless prepared many of the stages of the parchment themselves. The cottage industry of the monastic cloister left little scope for teams of professional collaborators. Even the parchment was doubtless a by-product of the monastery's kitchens, and paper was unknown. But certainly by the fourteenth century it seems to have been possible to purchase gatherings of parchment ready prepared for writing. Ruling continues under miniatures, and there is ruling on blank flyleaves. For many scribes, the task of writing a manuscript must have begun with neat stacks of paper or parchment gatherings, ready folded and ruled.

Before a scribe began to write, guide lines were ruled across the pages and their extremities were pricked through the margins, so that subsequent leaves could be ruled identically by joining up the prickings. (MS. Bodl. 270a, fol. 132r, England (possibly Yorkshire), third quarter of the twelfth century)

aliqui inimici non sequitur nouissima ini
mica. Cum hec destructa fuerit: immortali
tas succedit. Si nullus erit inimicus: quasi no
uissima destruetur mors. Bonum nrm cur si
speramus: pax erit. Ecce bonum fr̄s magnum
bonum pax uocatur. Querebatis quid uocaret.
Aurum est an argentum est. an fundus. an uestis.
Pax est. Non pax qualem inter se habent homi
nes. infidam. instabilem. mutabilem. incertam.
nec pax talis qualis secum habet ipse unus ho.
Diximus enim: quia & secum pugnat homo.
Usqequo domet omnes cupiditates: adhuc
pugnat. Qualis est pax. Quam oculus non uidit
nec auris audiuit. Qualis pax. De ierlm: quia
ierlm interpretatur uisio pacis. Sic & benedi
cat te dns ex syon. ut uideas que bona sunt ie
rlm. & uideas omnes dies uite tue & uideas n̄
filios tuos tantum. Sed filios filiorum tuorum.
Quid est filios tuos. Opa tua que tu agis. Qui sunt
filii filiorum. Fructus opum tuorum. Facis ele
mosinas. filii tui sunt. Propter elemosinas ac
cipis uitam eternam. filii filiorum tuorum sunt.
Videas filios filiorum tuorum. & erit quod seq̄r.
quod concluditur: pax super isrl. Hec pax pdicatur
nobis a nobis. Ipsa amatur a nobis ipsa ut ab
ametur optamus. Ad illam pacem puenimus.
qui & huc pacifici fuerint. Illi sunt & huc pacifici
qui & ibi. qui circumeunt mensam dni tanqua
nouella oliuarum. ut non sit sterilis arbor.
qualis fuit illa ficulnea ubi fructum non inue
nit esuriens dns. Et uideas. quid ei contigerit.
folia sola habebat: fructum non habebat. Sic
sunt qui uerba habent: & facta non habent.
Veniens esuriens dns. non ibi inuenit qd man
ducet: quia fidem nram & facta bona esurit
dns. Pascamus aut illum bene uiuendo: & pa
cem in eternum nobis uiuere donando. Expt
de psalmo. cxx. uii. Incipit
de psalmo. cxx. uiii.

Psalmus quem cantauimus
breuis est; sicut scriptum est
in euangelio de zacheo. statura
breuis & magnus in ope. sicut scriptum est de
illa uidua que duo minuta misit in gazo

philacium. breuis pecunia sed magna caritas.
sic & iste psalmus. si uerba numeres breuis est.
si sententias appendas: magnus est. Non q̄ non
poterit dicuns usque ad fastidium detinere.
Qua re aduertat prudentia uestra & assit in
tentio xpiana. Sonet uerbum di uolentibus
opportune nolentibus inportune. Inuenit
sibi locum. inuenit corda. ubi requiescat. in
uenit terram ubi germinet & fructum ferat.
Nam quia multi mali sunt & iniqui quos por
tat ecclesia usque infinem: manifestum est. Et
hi sunt quibus uerbum di superfluum est. & aut
sic in illos cadit. quom semen in uia concul
catur & a uolatilibus colligitur. aut sic in illos
cadit quom semen in petrosa loca ubi non
habet terram multam. statim exiit & tale
facto sole arescit. quia non habebat radice.
aut sic inter spinas quod & si germinet &
conetur in auras surgere. suffocatur tam
multitudine spinarum. Tales aut sunt q̄
uerbum di contempnunt sic uia. aut qui
ad horam gaudent. & facta tribulatione
sic est ut soli arescunt. aut qui cogitationibus
& curis & sollicitudine huius mundi. tanqua
spinis auaricie suffocant quod in illis cepat
germinare. Est aut etiam terra bona. quo se
men cum cecideret: affert fructum. aliud tri
cenum. aliud sexagenum. aliud centenum.
Siue parum siue multum. omnis in horreo eius.
Sunt q̄ tales. & propter hos loquimur. Prope
hos loquitur scriptura. propter hos non tacet
euangelisata. Sed illi audiant. ne forte aliud sint
hodie aliud cras. Ne forte mutentur audiendo.
aut arent uiam. aut lapides purgent. aut
spinas euellant. Dicat spō di. dicat nobis. can
tet nobis. Siue uolumus saltare siue nolumus
cantet ipse. Sicut enim qui saltat. membra
mouet ad cantum. sic q̄ saltant ad pceptum
di. opibus obtempant sono. Ideo qui noluerunt
hoc facere. quid illis dicet dns in euangelio.
Cantauimus uobis. & non saltastis. Planximus.
& non lamentastis. Cantet q̄. Credimus in
di misedia. quia erunt de quibus nos consola
tur. Nam qui pertinaces sunt & perseuerant in ma

imago pictorif eillum
nardus hui? opif.

II. INK AND SCRIPT

MANUSCRIPTS are written by hand. That is what the word means. Everyone is familiar with the image of the medieval scribe copying texts with a quill pen: it is quite correct. The inks were thicker and more glutinous than modern commercial ink, and there are numerous medieval recipes for their manufacture. We shall consider these in a moment. But there are no medieval instructions for the cutting of pens. There are allusions in Isidore of Seville, for instance, to the different nature of reed and quill pens in the seventh century, but nothing on their manufacture. All literate people evidently prepared their own pens and there was thus no merit in writing about how it was done. The cutting of a quill must have been entirely obvious and so familiar to every educated person from ancient Egypt to nineteenth-century England that it was not thought worthy of mention.

Modern scribes who use quill pens have evolved their own methods of preparing them, and these are likely to be as accurate for the Middle Ages as any historical research by reenactment can ever be. The best feathers prove to be the five or so outer wing pinions of goose or swan. Theophilus in the twelfth century asserted that goose quills were the best. It is sometimes claimed that the microscopic scripts of the university scribes were made with crow or raven quills. This is technically quite possible but a small pen is difficult to hold, especially if writing a Bible a thousand pages long, and tiny script may after all be the result of a bigger quill being cut to a finer tip. Turkeys, which produce

Hugo Pictor, the scribe and artist who signed a manuscript of a biblical commentary of Jerome, once at Exeter Cathedral. He shows himself ruling the manuscript with a knife and dipping his pen into an inkhorn. (MS. Bodl. 717, fol. 287v, Normandy, late eleventh century)

excellent quills, are native to America and were unknown in medieval Europe.

For a right-handed scribe a quill which fits most comfortably into the hand has a slight natural curve to the right. This, then, comes from the left wing of the bird. First of all, the thin end and most of the barbs would be trimmed or peeled away and most medieval pictures of scribes show simply the curved white barrel. Feathers freshly removed from the bird, or found on the beach, are too flexible and need hardening. They can either be left to dry out for some months or can be hardened artificially by soaking them in water and then plunging them for a few minutes into a tray of heated sand. The thin greasy outer skin and pith within the barrel can be scraped or rubbed away easily now. What remains is a tough and almost transparent tube. The tip is pared away on each flank

ABOVE: Medieval pens were usually quills, generally made from goose feathers hardened and cut to shape.

RIGHT: This frontispiece to the *Breviloquium* of Bonaventura shows a scribe cutting a quill; on his table are scissors and another knife. (MS. Canon. Misc. 265, fol. 12r, central Italy, third quarter of the fourteenth century)

Incipiunt capitula pmi libri.

Prima pars ð ciuitate ð̄. ḣt capt̃la. ix. ſ. ð q̄b̄ ē̄ theo̅ ī̄ ſu
Quid teneð ð ciuitate p̄ az ciuitate ccrine.
De iſtius fidei intllia ſana.
De iſtius fidei expſſē. catho̅

with a short and sharp knife – a penknife – usually in a double step, very much into the shape of a fountain pen nib. Then it is cushioned in the hand (rather like the action of peeling a potato) and a slit is cut up the centre of the nib. Finally the pen is laid with its nib against a firm surface and the scribe pushes down with the blade of his knife across the extreme end, removing a fraction of a millimetre to produce an absolutely clean crisp squared-off tip.

A modern scribe, demonstrating quill-cutting to a circle of admiring medievalists, can follow through these separate stages in a few moments of rapid scattering of parings. The medieval scribe doubtless prepared his pen at considerable speed and without great effort. The final cut across the tip has to be repeated quite often in the course of writing out a manuscript as the slit in the point will open up with use or with neglect. John of Tilbury, one of the scholars in the household of Thomas Becket in the twelfth century, describes how a clerk taking dictation would need to sharpen his pen so often that he had to have sixty or a hundred quills ready cut and sharpened in advance. The implication is that in the course of a day's work a busy scribe would sharpen his pen sixty times.

Medieval pictures of scribes in action are remarkably common, either as author portraits at the opening of their texts, or as part of the standard iconography of evangelists and of Saint Jerome in his study. Thus there are illustrations of people with pens from all periods of the Middle Ages. Especially in Books of Hours, which often open the section of Gospel Sequences with miniatures of the evangelists in the act of writing, we see the saints peering at their pens, sharpening them (pulling the blade towards them, not away as we might sharpen a pencil), scraping them with a knife, licking them, writing with them, propping them behind their ears and so forth, all intended to represent familiar homely activities of the manuscript maker. It is interesting, too, to notice how medieval

Saint Mark the evangelist sharpening a quill pen, before writing in a manuscript on his lap. (MS. Douce 31, fol. 19r, France (Bourges), second half of the fifteenth century)

writers are depicted holding their quills because it is not as we hold pens now. Most of us grasp writing implements between the tip of the forefinger and the first knuckle of the middle finger, secured firmly in place by the thumb. (Try it: it is easier than explaining.) The medieval scribe, to judge from pictures, held his pen pointing downwards on the inside of the tips of the middle and forefingers while holding it steady by the very tip of the thumb. The fourth and fifth fingers are curled up out of the way. In this way the quill meets the page much more vertically than a modern pen. Ink seems to flow better when a quill is at right angles to the page. The medieval practice of holding the quill gives less finger control than a modern pen and so movement comes from the whole hand. The quill itself, however, is infinitely lighter than a modern pen and it glides across the page without great effort. A proper understanding of the formation of medieval script should begin with some awareness that the pen was held differently.

The quills were what we would call dip-pens. A scribe cannot write without a pot of ink, and the miniatures of Saint John on Patmos sometimes include the figure of a mischievous devil who creeps up behind a bush with a grappling-hook to spirit away the saint's ink pot. This is an open-air scene and so the pot is portable, presumably with a screw lid, and it is attached by a cord to an oblong pencase. Not dissimilar pen and ink sets are used by Islamic scribes today, and doubtless it was a familiar image to the medieval scribe on the move. In the scriptorium ink was held in inkhorns; some scribes are shown holding these horns but usually both hands were occupied with knife and pen. Sometimes saints are shown with the good fortune of angels holding up their inkhorns in readiness. Evangelists depicted in Carolingian Gospel Books often have their ink on a separate stand, like a torchère, beside the desk (a sensible precaution if one is prone to knock the pot over). In late

The eagle of Saint John pecking at a devil who tries to steal the evangelist's inkpot and pencase to prevent him writing his Gospel. (MS. Douce 267, fol. 5r, France (Besançon), second half of the fifteenth century)

Jnuaum ści euuan
gelii secdm iohanne
N principio erat u
bum et uerbu erat

medieval pictures the horns are generally inserted into metal hoops attached into the edge of the right-hand side of the desk, and there are frequently two and sometimes three at once. There are examples where the horns are fitted into a vertical row of holes in the surface of the desk itself and their tips can be seen protruding below the table. In some manuscripts the inkhorn is shown conveniently inset into the arm of the scribe's chair.

There are a fair number of medieval recipes for making ink. There were two completely different types of black ink and it will be as well to distinguish between them at the outset. The first is carbon ink, made of charcoal or lamp-black mixed with a gum. The second is metal-gall ink, usually iron gall, made by mixing a solution of tannic acids with ferrous sulphate (*copperas*); it too requires added gum, but as a thickener rather than as an adhesive. The blackness is the result of a chemical reaction. Both types of ink were employed in medieval manuscripts. Carbon ink was used in the ancient and eastern worlds and occurs in all medieval recipes (there are many) until the twelfth century. This need not imply that it was the only method until that time, because accounts of craftsmanship in the earlier Middle Ages are more likely to retell a classical or literary source rather than to branch out into contemporary experience. There were certainly iron-gall inks in use by the third century, but there was no literary tradition of explaining them until Theophilus in the twelfth century. Thereafter, craftsmen's recipes describe gall inks, and undoubtedly most later medieval manuscripts are written with iron gall.

Its recipe is interesting, and it may come as a surprise to learn that a principal ingredient is the oak apple, that curious ball-like tumour, about the size of a small marble, which grows mainly on the leaves and twigs of oak trees. It is formed when a gall wasp lays its egg in the growing bud of the tree, and a soft pale-green

The Greek mathematician Pythagoras depicted by Matthew Paris as a scribe writing a manuscript, holding the page with a knife and dipping his pen into an inkpot kept safely distant. (MS. Ashmole 304, fol. 42r, England (St Albans), mid-thirteenth century)

Oak apples supply the principal ingredient of iron-gall ink: they are the nut-like growths on oak trees, formed when the gall wasp lays its eggs in the branches.

apple-like sphere begins to form around the larva. One can find galls quite easily on shrub oaks, even today, though the finest specimens were said to be those imported from Aleppo in the Levant. If picked too young, gall nuts shrivel up like rotten fruit; but when the larva inside is fully developed into an insect, it bores a hole out of its vegetable cocoon and it flies away and the hard nut which remains is rich in tannic and gallic acids. The galls are roughly crushed up and infused for some days in rainwater in the sun or by the fire. The physician Pietro Maria Canepario wrote in 1619 that this could be speeded up by boiling the crushed gall nuts for as long as it takes to recite the *Pater Noster* three times. Sometimes white wine or vinegar was used instead of rainwater. This, then, is the first ingredient of iron-gall ink. The second is ferrous sulphate, known also as *copperas*, green vitriol or *sal martis*. Both Dioscorides and Pliny write about copperas. It was manufactured or found naturally in Spain by the evaporation of water from ferrous earths. By the late sixteenth century, copperas was probably being made by pouring sulphuric acid over old nails, then filtering the liquid, and mixing the filtrate with alcohol (this may explain the acidity of post-medieval inks). The copperas is then added to the oak-gall potion, stirred in with a fig stick (according to Palatino in 1540, as if the ingredients were not obscure enough already); 'stere it ofte', said an English recipe of *c*. 1483. The resulting solution slowly turns from pale brown into black ink. Some ground-up gum arabic is added, not so much to supply adhesive but to make the ink thicker. Quill pens need the viscosity of gum; fountain pens, in fact, do not. Gum arabic, which we shall come to again in accounts of medieval pigments, is the dried-up sap of the acacia tree, brought to Europe from Egypt and Asia Minor. Ink-making is in many ways a wonderfully romantic process, redolent of alchemy.

Iron-gall ink darkens even further when exposed to air on the pages of a manuscript. It soaks well into parchment, unlike carbon inks which can be rubbed off relatively easily. It is more translucent and shinier than carbon ink which is grittier and blacker. Iron-gall ink was used for well over a thousand years, and Anglo-Saxon specimens have survived as crisply from the beginning of the period as Victorian inks from the end.

Medieval pictures of scribes, as mentioned above, sometimes show two inkhorns on the right of the desk. The second container was probably for red ink. Red was used greatly in medieval manuscripts, for headings, running-titles and initials, for rubrics (hence the word) in liturgical manuscripts, and in calendars for red-letter days (hence that term too). Corrections to the text were sometimes made in red, drawing attention to the care with which a text had been checked. Blue and green inks exist, but are rarer; red was always the second colour. We have the detailed account for the writing of a Gospel Lectionary by a canon of Windsor in 1380. Apart from the cost of labour and board and lodging for the scribe, the materials needed were itemised as parchment at 8d. a gathering, ink at 1s.2d., and vermilion at the comparatively high price of 9d. The vermilion is for red ink, and was a major ingredient in the contract. Red ink in manuscripts goes back at least to the fifth century and flourished until the fifteenth. It must have been the spread of printed books, in which producing coloured text is very complicated, which eroded the doubtless standard medieval assumption that books were artefacts in black and red. Printed books are simply black, which is duller. Vermilion is mercuric sulphide, and is blended into red ink by grinding up and mixing with white of egg and gum arabic. Red ink can also be made from brazilwood chips which were infused in vinegar or urine (apparently) and stirred in once more with gum arabic. Brazilwood, one should explain, is not a native of South America – the country was named after its abundance of the well-known trees already familiar to makers of medieval red ink.

One might suppose that once the scribe had assembled the ingredients, he would be ready to begin writing. There is, however, still a crucial piece of equipment without which almost no manuscript can be made. A scribe does not simply write: he copies and he must possess an exemplar from which to transcribe his text. This is already presupposing that the scribe has decided *which* text is to be copied next: that would make a fascinating study in its own

Red ink is used extensively for rubrics in liturgical manuscripts. (MS. Barlow 5, fol. 4r, England, early fifteenth century)

subdiacoꝰ casulis induantur
ad missam de die nisi in festis
scoꝝ et qñ missa Salus ꝑ
tuuo cũ dalmatica ꞇ tunica i
dui debent. ꝗ In missis uero
de uig ꞇ ieiuniis iiij.ᵒʳ tempoꝝ
geñaliter per totum añm in al
bis esse debent. nisi in uig pasch
et penteccostes et in uig naℓ dñi
quando contigit in dñica ꞇ iiij.ᵒʳ
tempoꝝ quando celebzatur in ebdõ
penteℓ. tunc dalmatica ꞇ tuni
ca induatur. Per reliquũ uero
tempus anni semper ad missam
dalmatica et tunica induantur
nisi in die parasℓ. et in rogacoĩbꝫ
ad missas ieiunii et ꝓcessionũ
ꞇ in dñicalibꝫ missis ꞇ scoꝝ que
in capitulo dicantur ꞇ in missis
ꝓ defunctis tunc in albis cũ amic
tibus esse tenentur. ꝗIn die ta
men cõmemoracoĩs ꝯax et in
missis pro corpore presenti et in
anniũsariis epoꝝ ꞇ diaconoꝝ ec
clie sarum dalmaticis ꞇ tunicis
induanꞇ. Et sciendum est qd
per totum aduentũ et a lxx. ul
ꝙ ad cenam dñi missa cũ. Gñdi
camus dño. finiatur. per totũ
annũ generalis haℓetur regula
qd semper quando ad missam dℓ

deus meus in te
confido non e
rubescam. neꝙ
irrideant me
inimici mei. ete
nim uniũsi qui te expectant nõ cõ
fundentur. ℣ Uias tuas dñe
demonstra michi: et semitas tuas
edoce me. Repetatur offiñ secd ꞇ
postea dr. Glia pñ ꞇ Sicut erat
tercio repetatur offiñ. et hoc per
totũ annũ obseruetur tam in dõ
cis qñ in fis scoꝝ ꞇ in oct et in
fra qñ choꝝus regitur ꞇ in omnibꝫ
missis de sca maꝛ per totũ añm
nisi a dñica passionis dñi usꝙ
ad cenam dñi. s. ad missam de
temporali tñ. Per totũ aduentũ
non dr Glia in excelsis. de quociũ
ꝙ dicatur missa. ꝗHijs itaꝙ ꝑ
actis: scd ꝙ signaculo crucis in
facie sua uertat se sacℓ ad ꝓpłm
elenatis ꝙ aliquatulũ brachijs
iunctis ꝙ manibꝫ dic hoc m.

Crustũ re
uitat se ad
Dñs uobñ. altaꝛ ꞇd. Oremꝫ
Exrata qñs dñe ꝓ oꝛ
uoluntatem tuam ꞇ nei
uit ab iminentibꝫ ꝑcoꝝ
noꝝum uigiliis: te mereꞇ

right, if only enough evidence could be assembled on the motives for selecting texts and on the order in which desiderata were tackled.

If the scribe were a monk, working only for his monastery's own library, there might be little urgency to reproduce a text already represented in the collection, but if the text was not in the library there is then the even more intriguing problem of how the scribe knew about the text anyway (especially a new work by a distant author) and, if he did find references to it elsewhere, of how he was able to borrow an exemplar to copy. Answers to these questions take us right to the heart of intellectual and cultural history and have to be beyond the scope of this book. There was evidently a surprising amount of travel between one monastery and another, and a great deal of carrying about of manuscripts. There exist early Irish manuscripts with contemporary ownership inscriptions of German abbeys, Parisian university manuscripts from the libraries of remote English monasteries, Italian legal manuscripts which wandered when newly written into France, and so forth. There are also letters from one abbey to another, either requesting the favour of having a text copied and sent, or asking if exemplars could be made available. Nonetheless, it is a tantalising question, and glimpses from thousand-year-old monastic correspondence or apparent textual links between surviving manuscripts supply only a partial answer.

By the time of the secular workshops of the Gothic period it was not necessarily easier to find exemplars because of the infinitely greater number of texts in circulation. Surely texts like Bibles in the thirteenth century and Books of Hours in the fifteenth century, which were the stock-in-trade of medieval booksellers, were copied from exemplars owned on the premises. It may be that some of the grubbier surviving copies served their time as exemplars in

Copying an earlier manuscript was not always easy. A later scribe, confronting this manuscript of Latin grammar, might find it almost impossible to distinguish the original text from its later additions and notes. (MS. Auct. T. 2. 20, fol. 11v, France (possibly Auxerre), ninth century)

DE VERBO

Verbum + parsorationis cum tem
pore & psona sinecasu ut agere
aliquid aut pati aut neutrum signif
cans. Verbo accidunt VII qualitas

coniugatio Genus numerus figura

the Middle Ages, but no indisputable exemplar is known for either text. Sometimes, no doubt, a customer simply walked into the scribe's shop with a manuscript under his arm and commissioned a copy. Most of the very early booksellers and professional scribes were concentrated in the university towns and exemplars were certainly more easily available in Paris or Oxford, for example, than in provincial villages.

One of the earliest recognisably professionally made manuscripts from Paris is a copy of Ptolemy in the Bibliothèque nationale de France with an inscription recording its completion in December 1213 from an exemplar in the abbey library of St-Victor in Paris, and by chance the St-Victor copy of the same text still survives and is now also in the Bibliothèque nationale, allowing us to place the monastic original and the secular copy side by side again more than eight hundred years later. The humanists raided monastic libraries in their search for lost classical texts, carrying off the originals to use as exemplars, if they were allowed, or copying the texts *in situ*, if they were not. In the thirteenth and fourteenth centuries, certain university towns, mainly Paris and Bologna, operated a kind of exemplar loan service whereby a wide range of student textbooks could be hired out for copying a gathering at a time. Each of these gatherings was known as a *pecia* and could be rented from an authorised university stationer. There were published lists of the texts available and the cost of hiring each part of the exemplars. There are many complications in interpreting the mechanics of the *pecia* system (and it is not appropriate now to delve into its remarkable ramifications as this would distract the story even further from the actual process of book production) but one must accept that the keeping, borrowing, begging or hiring of exemplars was an important preliminary to the business of writing a medieval book.

Jean Miélot (d. 1472) was a scribe in the court of the dukes of Burgundy and is shown here copying a text from an exemplar propped open before him. (Paris, Bibliothèque nationale de France, MS. fr. 9198, fol. 19r, southern Netherlands, third quarter of the fifteenth century)

Roys, Maistre prenez repos solacieux, En
te saint lit jours sepmaines et moys, Coe
en celluy qui fu tresdesireux, Lit prepare
au fil du roy des roys,

Sensieut ung petit prologue sur l'assuptio de la vierge
marie, trislate de latin en frucois, Par Jo. Milot

A letus scruteur de ihucrist en leglise
de sarde Ases venerables fres e miss
Demourans a ladene salut Je me
ramembre bien que jay souuent escript

There are at least two portraits of the Flemish scribe Jean Miélot in manuscripts of the third quarter of the fifteenth century. Both show the exemplar propped open on a lectern just above the scribe's own sloping writing desk. The lectern appears to be double-sided and supported by a metal swivel attached to his own desk so that Miélot could move it round to just above his eye level while copying and could presumably rotate it to compare another exemplar on the back or could swing the entire lectern out of the way. It looks very ingenious and may contain an element of wishful fantasy. The evangelist and author portraits we considered earlier for their depiction of scribes are less helpful in showing exemplars because in divine revelation there is supposed to be no exemplar at all. Saint Gregory is often shown writing as the Holy Dove whispers in his ear. Both the exemplar and the copy were usually simply placed side by side on a sloping desk. We can see in miniatures that manuscripts were held open by weights hanging from each end of a string, with one end dangling over the back of the desk and the other hanging down across the top of the page. A parchment manuscript will tend to close itself up unless it is held open. Sometimes the weights are shown as more or less triangular with rounded tops and extended horizontal lower edges. As the scribe copied a text, it would be relatively easy to pull the weight down the page so that the long horizontal edge of the weight would very effectively mark his exact place in the exemplar.

Scribes sat very upright, often on tall-backed chairs (to judge from pictures again) or on benches, before sloping desks. Some medieval illustrations show the desk top actually attached to the chair, apparently hinging up to let the scribe sit down and then falling down again into place, rather like a baby's highchair. Looking at the pictures, however, it is difficult to envisage how the scribe wriggled into the seat; even with the hinge up. A bench has the advantage for a scribe that he can slide himself along it as he works, which is less tiring than forever twisting his whole body back and forth. The slope of the desk is quite steep. As mentioned, quill pens are most effective when held at right angles to the writing surface, and this is easier to achieve on an angled desk. It also means that the pen is held very gently sloping downwards, allowing controlled flow of ink. The way we hold pens today requires the the edge of the hand to rest on the page while manipulating the fingers, but a pen held as described earlier scarcely requires the hand to touch the page at all, and movement is from the arm. For this, the flexibility of a sloping desk is ideal. As ink takes some moments to dry, one can sometimes see on the pages of medieval manuscripts that the concentration of ink is in the lower edges of the letters as it has settled down the slope of the desk.

As the scribe sat down to commence copying, he was recommended by the recipes to give his parchment a final rub over with fine pumice and to smooth the surface off with chalk. This was to remove any grease stains that may have come about in handling and folding the sheets, and to reduce the risk of the ink running. He probably tried out the pen with a few words on a scrap of parchment. One sometimes sees phrases on flyleaves such as 'probatio penne', or 'Edwardus dei gratia rex', as meaningless as 'testing, 1-2-3' over a loudspeaker at sports' day, or invocations such as 'assit principio meo ihesus maria' (or 'franciscus', perhaps if it was a Franciscan scribe) written in tiny script along the very upper margin of the first page. As he actually wrote, the scribe held a knife in his left hand. This is important, and universal in the Middle Ages. Writing, like eating, was a two-handed operation. It meant, among other things, that he had no spare hand for following his place in the exemplar. The knife was for sharpening the pen and for erasing mistakes (quickly, before the ink had really soaked in) and, more

practically, for holding down the always springy surface of the vellum, moving along the line as the scribe wrote each word. To steady the page with the finger is potentially greasy and clumsy, but a knife tip gives precision and control.

This is not the place to write a history of medieval script. It is a subject which becomes more and more complicated with greater experience. A scribe working alone at his desk had no notion that his own script was part of a continuing evolution. He would in any case have been capable of several contemporaneous scripts appropriate to the text he was writing: display script for headings, grand noble letters for Missals, quick cursive hands for vernacular literature, charter hands for documents and so on. Analysis of major early monastic manuscripts sometimes reveals evidence of what seem to have been master and pupil scribes. A good scribe starts the book, and then a less competent hand writes some paragraphs, then the first hand returns (as if demonstrating and re-emphasising some point), and then back comes the trainee with a longer stint, and so on, until the whole book is finished by the pupil in what is perhaps his qualifying piece. House styles of script were in this way passed on from one generation to the next, but were so contaminated by other influences (including the exemplar, so often from elsewhere) that only rarely can a manuscript be attributed to a particular workshop on script alone.

One cannot generalise about how individual letter-forms were drawn. It is usually easier to pull a quill pen downward on a page than to push it up, and so round shapes like 'o' would be simpler to execute with two or more down-strokes than one circular loop; but so much depends on the particular script being written. If one looks carefully at the individual letters of any manuscript, especially with pencil in hand, it is not difficult to establish to one's own satisfaction the order in which individual strokes were made.

A specimen sheet of the different kinds of script which a single professional scribe could offer to clients. (MS. e Mus. 198*, fol. 8r, England (possibly Oxford), fourteenth century)

et dixit eis nolite metuere ... dño nobis qma ...

im iam uiuit z uita hominū cū eo surrexit alle

aduiuata a dñi

lo in confessio ne

...iu me sal uam fe cit

est me. Cuitans

ihū xpiste qui misisti ad me.

Symeon ille senex dñm inte
compatur anne: z audierat
eēt iusurus morte. nisi uiderit
gte fres qñtum desideriū ha
bēt: uidere xpiū. Haebant ill
rōm qui pie uiuebūt. dicebāt
At illa natiuitas? O si q cred
tiuus dei uideam oclis meis
amaquos scōs z uirtps oste
cessū est. hic symeoni. dūs
dicat. qm ulta uidi z ipse noli
nos uidetis: z nō uiderūt. Et
uitas: z nō audierūt. hic ū
cessū erut uiam deceptus qñ d
ti cotidie in oraōnibz suis.

...scet: putas diuabz: dure
...dcnibz siuis. z p desiderio su

: fidelium deus
conditor z rede

Mimicking medieval hands is a diverting pastime. A convincing forgery of a whole book would be so difficult to achieve that imitation is a pastime which runs little risk of criminal temptation.

Professional Gothic scribes were capable of producing several scripts, and a number of display posters have been discovered demonstrating ranges of hand which the scribe could offer to clients. Pieces of an early fourteenth-century parchment poster have been found as part of the stiffening inside a bookbinding made in Oxford around 1340. The fragments come from a single sheet, written on one side only in a whole range of different Gothic scripts, and they are stained and weathered. The supposition is that the poster was once tacked up outside a stationer's shop (presumably in Oxford) until it became obsolete or was replaced and so was taken down and stored as a useful scrap of thick parchment. One day its pieces proved ideal for padding out a binding, and thus the oldest known English public advertisement has come down to us. It shows short specimens of twelve different scripts for different classes of liturgical manuscript, from a large choir psalter to little portable processionals with music. There are similar Continental specimens from the fifteenth century, advertising the range of hands available from the scribes Herman Stepel, of Münster in Westphalia, for example, or Robert of Tours, in the diocese of Nantes. Presumably the customer came into the shop, looked over the patterns as one might a menu in a takeaway restaurant, and left an order for a particular script.

A commercial scribe charged by the gathering. There are interesting accounts for making manuscripts in a cache of six fifteenth-century English manuscripts in Peterhouse in Cambridge. They are big thick manuscripts of St Augustine and St Jerome. Each ends with an itemised breakdown of the cost, so much for parchment, so much for writing the text, so much for illumination,

and so much for the binding, with a total price. Vellum is 3d. a
gathering for books under twelve inches (30 cm) high (MSS 110, 142,
154, 193 and 198) and 6d. a gathering for the one larger book (MS 88).
The writing is 16d. a quire for the five smaller books and 20d. a
quire for the bigger one. The binding up of the gatherings cost 2s.
and 2s.6d., according to size. The same price of 20d. a gathering
was charged for the writing of a Psalter bought by the Paston
family in 1467.

The gathering was the unit of production and the scribe on
completion of his task would have a stack of separate quires ready
to be divided among the illuminators or sent away to be bound.
It was obviously very important that the gatherings should be
kept in order or be capable of reassembly in sequence without
risk of confusion. The earliest western manuscripts had their
gatherings numbered on the last page of each, either numerically
or alphabetically, A, B, C and so forth, sometimes preceded by
'Q' (quaternion). This served its purpose splendidly in the ages of
monastic book production when work was leisurely and in-house
and there was little danger of confusing the gatherings of one
manuscript with those of another. But by the twelfth century, as
manuscript production became a larger enterprise, scribes adopted
catchwords instead, writing them in the lower inner corner of
the last page of each gathering. A catchword anticipates the first
word of the following gathering. A binder simply has to match up
each catchword with its twin at the top of the next gathering to
assemble the book in its correct sequence. In any handmade book,
the exact number of words a scribe will have copied over sixteen
pages will vary from one transcript to another, and thus even if
(by chance) a shop was preparing several copies of the same text
in the same format at the same time and even if all the gatherings
were muddled up, it would still be possible to put them back in

The catchword '[pre]sidium', written decoratively within a king's crown, at the end of a gathering of a Missal copied by the scribe Alexander de Pulesdon; it is also marked 'cor' showing that it was corrected quire by quire. (MS. Barlow 5, fol. 180v, England, early fifteenth century)

es tu: et ppter nomen tuum deduces me
et enutries me.

El duces me de laqueo quem absconde
runt m̄: qm tu es protector meus

In manus tuas domine comendo spi
ritum meum redemisti me domine deus
ueritatis.

Odisti obseruantes uanitates: sup̄ uacue.

Ego autem in domino speraui 7 exulta
bo: et letabor in misedia tua.

Qm respexisti humilitate meam: salua
sti de necessitatibz aiam meam.

Nec conclusisti me in manibz inimia:
statuisti in loco spacioso pedes meos.

Qm defecit in dolore uita mea 7 anni
mei in gemitibz:

Infirmata est in paupptate uirtus mea

Miserere mei dūe qm tribulor: conturbatus est ocu
lus meus aia mea et uenter meus.

order because every pair of catchwords would be unique to that copy. Sometimes catchwords were decorated, and usually they were horizontal but fifteenth-century Italian examples were sometimes vertical. Much depended on the whim of the scribe, and to note the form of catchwords is one method of beginning to distinguish the work of individual scribes.

When a manuscript was finished, the text was usually checked for errors, either by the scribe himself or by a colleague. It is very difficult to copy without making some mistakes, and very many pages of medieval manuscripts show evidence of corrections, either by erasing and rewriting words, or by inserting omissions in margins, or by crossing out repetitions. Some of the most common are caused by eye-skip. A scribe copies out a sentence and looks back at the exemplar, bearing in mind the last letters he has just written, and his eye settles on another word which ends the same way and he begins copying from there in error. In Latin, as it happens, many words have the same endings, especially verbs which finish sentences, and so this is a real risk. In some manuscripts which the scribe did not expect the client to read very carefully and which were as much for show as use, there was a scribal custom of adding discreet rows of dots under words or phrases which ought not to be there. It indicated that the scribe was aware of the mistake but that everyone agreed it would be a shame to spoil the handsome look of the page with an erasure or deletion. There are examples of this endearing practice throughout the Middle Ages.

The final words that a scribe wrote in a manuscript may simply be the end of the text. Frequently there is an *explicit*, announcing that this is the conclusion of such-and-such a text, very often with the name of the author. Occasionally the scribe signs the book. Scribal signatures are not as rare as one might suppose. Over the recent decades the Benedictine monks of Le Bouveret in Switzerland

In this Psalter the scribe omitted a verse and then added it in the lower margin, keyed in by a red cross beside an ape ringing church bells. (MS. Douce 118, fol. 35v, France (Artois), late thirteenth century)

subiecerat deuitus. s; cum ppha dm scepto in hac re
partuiss; conceptum ex ea filium iezrael pcipitur
nominare do pollutente post breue tempus sangnem
iezrael in domo seu uindicari. cui pmissionis hec
ca e. seu pheliseum i regno unctum ad uindicandum
sanguinem naboth cuis iezrael q tunc erat met
polis quem iezabel achab regis ist uxor intem te
sicut historia regum exponit. Is cum guut iux di
uinum pceptum uindicandi sangnis ca i omne
memorati domu deseluss; s pacto dni deliq ille i
uenitur. cuius pnepote ieroboam qui icone comp
hsus e originis sue tra imitante aco di scepta et
religionem cu populo ist agnte. sanguis naboth
qui in lco icte iezrael fiat pfusus. i domo seu pns me
morati ieroboam peta redundaturus significatur.
hinc scm e in ira dei in populum ist p redundacom
ppe pcessura dicetur. domus au uida mia icone co
prehensa ob h pmissa e. qp ezechias rex iuda filium
achaz sublatis ydol qtam pr eius et ceti reges con
sectauunt. templum dei purgasse ac purificasse mss

R V.

domini q factum est ad
olee filium beeri in diebz
ozie ioatham achaz eze
chie regum iuda. z in di
ebz ieroboam filii ioas re
gis ist. principium loq
i domino in osee. et di
xit dominus ad osee. vade sume t uxorem fornica
riam z fac filios fornicationum. qp fornicans forni
cabit trra domino. Et abiit z accepit gomer filiam
debelaim z concepit z pepit ei filium. Et dix domin
ad eum uoca nomen eius iezrael. qm adhuc modi
cum z uisitabo sangnem iezrael supra domum ieu
z quiece faciam regnum domus ist. Et in illa die
conteram arcum ist in ualle iezrael. Et conceptit
adhuc z pepit filiam. Et dix ei uoca nomen eius ab
sq mia. qp non addam ultra misereri domui ist.
s obliuione obliuiscar eorum z domui iuda mise

qm in er tunc mag q num
ei frumitum z uinum z oleum
caui ei z auu q fecunt baal su
strumitum meu in tpr suo z u
liberabo lanam meam z linu z
niam ei z nuc reuelabo stultici
euis turn n eruet eam de mani
omnie gaudium ei sollempint
omnia festa z ipra eius z comi
us de quibz dix q hedes hee mer
matores mei z ponam eam in
a agri z uisitabo sup eam dies
bat in censum z ornabatur in
uibar post amatores suos z me
dominus. ipsa h ecce ego laca
in solitudinem z loquar ad co
res eius ex eodem loco z uallen
z canet ibi iux dies iuuentuti
tis sue z iux dies ascensionis sue
die illa ait dominus uocabit n
me ultra baalim. z auferam no
et nt recordabitur ultra nomin
tedus in die illa cam bestia a
reptili trre z cum z gladium
et dormire eos faciam fiducial
spitum. et sponsabo te m i
i miseracionibz. Et sponsabo te
do. Et erit in die illa exaudiar
am celos z illi exaudient trra
z uinum z oleum z hec exaudient
am im in terram z miserebor
cam non populo meo ipse mi
z dix dominus ad me. Adhuc
mulierem dilectam amico z a
uoc ist. z ipsi respiciunt ad deo
unada uuarum. z fodi eam z
ordei z dimidio choro ordei. Et
ris expectabis me. son fornic
go expectabo te. qp dies mul
rege z sine princip. z sine sacrificio
z sine triaphim. et post hec reue
rentur dominum deum suu

LEFT: Here at Hosea 1:2 in a Bible, the scribe copied God's distressing injunction to the prophet to take a whore as a wife, 'uxorem fornicariam', then deleted part of the last word by underlining it with dots, and corrected it in the margin to 'uxorem fornicationum', a more correct reading. (MS. Auct. D. 3. 5, fol. 197v, England (possibly Oxford), mid-thirteenth century)

ABOVE: *Homeoteleuton* is a mistake caused by the scribe's eye jumping to a different occurrence of the same word. Here in a Bible he copied '... etiam mittentis', paused, looked back at the exemplar and lighted on another 'mittentis' five words later, and continued from there, missing out a whole phrase, later reinserted. (MS. Canon. Bibl. Lat. 52, fol. 498v, France (Paris), mid-thirteenth century)

De iuramento votorum.

Utrum votum obediencie sit potissimum inter tria vota.

Utrum religiosi si peccant mortaliter transgrediendo ea que sunt regule.

Utrum religiosus eodem genere peccati gravius peccet quam secularis.

De operibus Religiosorum. Questio 187. De hiis que competunt religiosis.

Utrum liceat religiosis docere predicare et huiusmodi facere.

Utrum liceat eis de negociis secularibus se intromittere.

Utrum teneantur manibus operari.

Utrum liceat eis de elemosinis vivere.

Utrum liceat eis mendicare.

Utrum liceat eis vilia vestimenta deferre.

De diversitate religionum. Questio 188. De differencia religionum.

Utrum sint diverse religiones vel una tantum.

Utrum aliqua religio institui possit ad opera vite active.

Utrum aliqua religio ordinari possit ad militandum.

Utrum aliqua religio institui possit ad predicandum vel confessiones audiendas.

Utrum possit aliqua religio institui ad studium littere.

Utrum religio que ordinatur ad vitam contemplativam sit potior ea que ordinatur ad vitam activam.

Utrum esse ad solos divites sit de perfectione religionis.

Utrum religio solitariorum sit preferenda religioni in societate viventium.

De ingressu religionis. Questio 189. De hiis que pertinent ad religionis ingressum vel ad eum ingredientes.

Utrum ille qui vovet religionem ingredi teneatur perpetuo in religione manere.

Utrum pueri sint recipiendi ad religionem.

Utrum aliquis debeat voto se astringere ad religionem ingrediendam vel obsequendam.

Utrum plures curas possint licere religionem intrare.

Utrum liceat de una religione transire ad aliam.

Utrum liceat alium inducere aliis ad ingrediendum religionem.

Utrum aliquem liceat religionem intrare absque multorum consilio.

Explicit secunda pars summe fratris thome de Aquino ordinis fratrum predicatorum longissima prolixissima et tediosissima scribenti. Deo gratias. Deo gratias. item Deo gratias.

have been publishing their vast index of colophons of signed
medieval manuscripts and their list, which is far from exhaustive,
records nearly 19,000 signatures of scribes in colophons of medieval
manuscripts. The old image of the anonymous craftsman needs to
be re-thought. Some scribes simply sign themselves Johannes, or
Rogerius, which tells us very little. A reasonable number are women,
which one might not have expected. Some names reappear often
enough that one can start to plot careers of professional scribes,
especially in fifteenth-century Italy. Quite often medieval scribes
were not full-time copyists of books. They may have been owners
making books for personal use, or notaries, students between
lectures, moonlighting royal clerks, parish priests unable to live
on their stipends, inmates of the debtors' prison, and so forth.
Perusing through the volumes of colophons gives glimpses of
human life on every page. The most amusing colophons in medieval
manuscripts are those in which a scribe triumphantly declares his
delight in completing the task, often to a formula of complaining
of the length of the book or asking for eternal life, or a good jug of
wine or a pretty girl.

On completing this volume
of Aquinas the scribe
records that it was the
'longest, most extensive
and most boring to write:
Thank God, thank God,
and once again thank God'
(New College MS. 121,
fol. 367v, scribe's colophon,
England (possibly Oxford),
early fourteenth century)

Na autem sabbati uenerunt de
luculo admonumentum maria mag
dalena & altera maria & quaedam cum eis
portantes quae parauerunt aromata &
inuenerunt lapiden reuolutum amonumento
Et ingresse noninuenerunt corpus dñ·
Et factum est dum mente consternate esse
ut deisto· Ecce duo uiri steterunt secus illas
inueste fulgenti· Cum uiderent timerent adecli
uarent uultum interra· Dixerunt ad illas·
quid queritis uiuentem cum mortuis non
est hic sed surrexit· Rementbramini qualiter
locutus est uobis cum adhuc ingalilea esse
dicens quia oporte filium hominis tradi
inmanus hominum peccatorum &crucifigi
& tertia die resurgere· Et recordate sunt
uerborum horum & regresse amonumen
to nuntiauerunt haec omnia illis xi & ce
teris omnibus· Erat autem maria mag

III. ILLUMINATION AND BINDING

MOST MEDIEVAL MANUSCRIPTS are decorated. Not every volume includes the richly illuminated borders and miniatures, which to many people are the great delight of manuscripts, but it is unusual for a completed medieval book to comprise nothing but script. From late antiquity there had been a custom of enlarging the first letter and filling it in with colour, and the earliest Irish manuscripts at the beginning of the seventh century already show text divided into sections marked out by big penwork initials ornamented with interlaced patterns and simple animal forms. For the next eight hundred years even the humblest text manuscripts usually opened with enlarged initials on the first pages, and they indicated chapters or other subdivisions in the text with similar but slightly smaller capitals. Medieval books have no title pages. The opening initial has the practical function of introducing or announcing the beginning.

In the early Irish manuscripts the initial of the first word is very big, the next letter is not quite so large, the next slightly smaller again, and so on, diminishing down letter by letter to the size of the text itself. So too throughout medieval manuscripts there are initials of different sizes, depending on their position and function in the text. This is what is often referred to as the hierarchy of decoration, and it is an appropriate word for the Middle Ages when people had a strong sense of the gradation of things. Angels, stars, animals, kingdoms, officers of church and state, feudal households and so on, were all classified into levels of unalterable rank and status with much more assurance than today,

Even the earliest manuscripts were decorated. Ornamented openings in Irish manuscripts began with large initials gradually diminishing in size in the opening words of the text. (MS. Rawl. G. 167, fol. 60v, Ireland, eighth century)

and a similar hierarchical sense of the order of things is inherent in the ornamentation of texts. This may sound complicated, but it is actually quite important. If, for example, we are confronting manuscript Bibles or Books of Hours or illustrated literary texts, which have many component parts, we can only begin to judge the design when we realise that in selecting ornaments the makers have deliberately apportioned levels of status and subdivision to each section.

There is a whole range of choices for decoration from lavish full-page miniatures, or even cycles of miniatures, down to small initials in red or blue or capital letters splashed with a dab of red or yellow. There can be partial or full borders and these can be quite simple or joyously crammed with ivy leaves and acanthus scrolls with birds, rabbits, monkeys and grotesques. Decoration can be in full colour, with or without gold, on the first page only or throughout the manuscript. It is sometimes in austere monochrome, especially grey, in a style known as *grisaille*. It is quite impossible to summarise the infinite possibilities, and part of the real delight of handling medieval manuscripts is that every one is different. But within each manuscript, one should stress again, there are pre-determined and recognisable gradations of ornament.

In the York Chapter Acts for 26 August 1346 there is the record of a scribe Robert Brekeling appearing before the cathedral chapter and confirming under oath to keep his contract to make for his client John Farbor a manuscript Psalter and Office of the Dead with a Hymnary and Collectar. The hierarchy of illumination is laid down precisely. The initials for psalms 1 and 109 are to be six or seven lines high (these, it happens, are the opening psalms for Matins and Vespers on Sundays). The initials marking each nocturn are to be five lines high. Each psalm and every double feast in the Hymnary and Collectar is to begin with a big initial in gold on a

The different sizes of the initials in a Psalter (here five lines high, three lines or one line) are a way of indicating the relative gradation of different components of the text. (MS. Auct. D. 4. 4, fol. 204r, England, second half of the fourteenth century)

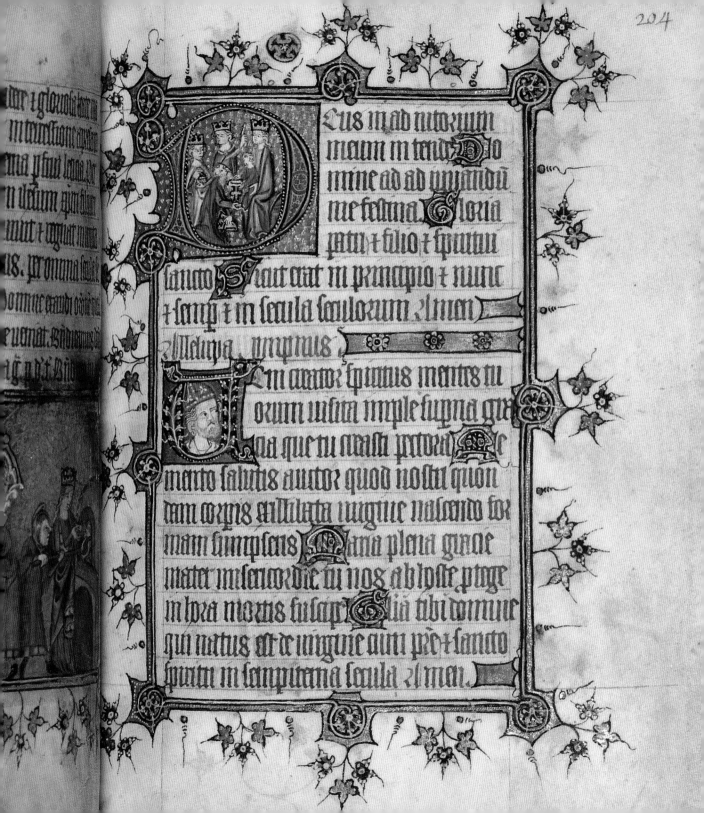

Eus in adiutorium
meum intende Do
mine ad adiuuandū
me festina Gloria
patri + filio + spiritu
sancto Sicut erat in principio + nunc
+ semp + in secula seculorum Amen
Alleluya. Hympnus

Eni creator spiritus mentes tu
orum uisita imple supna gra
tia que tu creasti prctora De
mento salutis autor quod nostri quon
dam corpis ex illibata i uirginie nascendo for
mam sumpsens Maria plena gratie
mater misericordie tu nos ab hoste protege
in hora mortis suscipi Gloria tibi domine
qui natus est de uirginie cū patre + sancto
spiritu in sempiterna secula Amen.

Occasionally instructions to an illuminator survive in the margins of manuscripts, revealing medieval terms for the different sizes of illuminated initial, '*champe*' for small one and '*sprynget*' for a larger initial with flourishing. (MS. Laud Misc. 253, fols. 214v and 253r, England, third quarter of the fifteenth century)

Custodiat te ihc xpc. amē.
Confortet te spūs sanctus. Amen.
Prestet tibi victoriam triuus et
vnus deus qui viuit ⁊ regnat per oīa
scła scłorum. Amen. De iudicio oculorum
infirmorum quā magr̄ Willm̄ de morti-
bz matris ecclie lincolnieñs. cancellari
instituit. cū necessitas inducat ⁊ de-
uocio postulancium vollūt hoc modo.

Domine ihū xpe qui aperuisti
oculos cci nati sana huius
famuli tui oculos daus in eis visū
pspicacem sufficientem ⁊ donecum ⁊
competantem in obsequiū tuum per
virtutem huius sacrii amēti et ⁊ hoc sig-
nū sancte crucis tue. ✠ In noīe pris.
⁊ cc̄. Et tūo signo crucis sac signet eū
cū corporalibz ⁊ asdē vertiletr i oculis
eī cū dicat In noīe pris ⁊ f. ⁊ s. s. a.

Ordo ad visitandum in-
firmū. In pmis induat
se sac in superpell cū sto-
la ⁊ in eundo cum suis
ministris dicat vii. psos penit. cum.
Glia pri. ⁊ Sicut erant, vna cū a. Ne
reminiscaris. Et sciendū est qd̄ hoc
sacrm̄ amētū fuit institutū a dn̄o tunc

Dmine labia mea aperies. Et os meum annuncabit

multicoloured ground. Ordinary feasts in the Hymnary and Collectar are to open with enlarged initials in gold and red. The small versal initials of every psalm are to be in blue and red throughout. All this was prescribed before the work began. John Farbor was evidently one of those customers who liked to know exactly what he was getting for the 16s.9d. that this book was estimated to cost.

The processes of making a medieval manuscript fall into clear stages. It has long been recognised that the decoration has to be added subsequent to the writing of the text (it would be exceedingly difficult the other way around). Therefore the script is supplied first, and blank spaces are left for the decoration. This presupposes very careful planning by the scribe even before he puts pen to parchment. Some manuscripts survive unfinished and show exactly this: the script in irregular blocks with blank spaces parcelled out for the insertion of pictures or initials. Often even completed manuscripts reveal traces of plummet lines marking off compartments which were subsequently filled with ornament. This may seem self-evident, perhaps, but it emphasises the important fact that decisions on the hierarchy of decoration, on the size and extent of the miniatures, on the richness and scale of the whole book were all settled and irrevocable long before the illuminator was subcontracted into the operation. It is too easy to consider a famous illuminated manuscript as representing the design genius and originality of a particular artist, or to try to link the subject matter of the pictures with his creative personality or initiative. We easily classify manuscripts as being representative of the workshop of the Boucicaut Master, for example, or from the circle of Jean Pucelle, or from the shop of the Master of Petrarch's Triumphs. It was entirely the other way round. Illumination in commercially made manuscripts would undoubtedly have been discussed

Unfinished manuscripts show that the miniatures were added last, or perhaps sometimes by different artists, as in this French Book of Hours. (MS. Douce 267, fol. 114r, France (Besançon), third quarter of the fifteenth century)

Incipit prephatio vene-
rabilis BEDE presbiteri.
in uitam beati patris
CVTHBERTI lindisfarnensis ep̄i.

DOMINO AC BEATISSIMO
patri EADFRIDO ep̄o. &
omni congregationi fr̄m̄ q̄
in lindisfarnensi insula
xp̄o deseruiunt. beda fidel-
is coseruus salutem. Quia ius-
sistis dilectissimi. ut libro que
de uita beate memorie patris nr̄i
CVTHBERTI uiro rogatu coposui. pfationem aliq̄ in fron-
te iuxta morem ipsigerem. p̄qua legentibus uniuersis & ur̄e
uoluntatis desideriu. & obedientionis nr̄e patrit assensio
sina claresceret. placuit incapite pfationis & uob
q̄nostis ad memoriam reuocare. & eis q̄ignorant hec
forte legentibus notu facere. qa necsine certissima in-
q̄sitione reru gestaru. aliqd detanto uiro scribe. nectan-
de ea que scripseram sine subtili examinatione testiu
in dubioꝛ pūssī transcribenda qbꝫ da dare ꝑsupsisse:
qn potiꝰ p̄mo diligent exordiu. pgressu. & terminu glo-
sissime cu satione acurte illa abhis q̄nouerant. in-
uestigasse. Quoꝛ etiā nomina inipso libro aliquoti-
ens obcertu cognite ueritatis indiciu apponenda iu-
dicaui. & sic denium ad scedulas manum mittere

initially between the patron and the scribe (or the scribe's agent), but by the time that the written gatherings were sent off to the illuminator there was no longer any scope for innovation.

As they wrote out manuscripts, scribes sometimes went further than simply leaving spaces. Guide letters were written in tiny script for the initials, and perhaps initials themselves were lightly sketched if the shape was unusual, like a long 'V' tapering into the text or a 'Q' with a tail intruding across the page. Written orders for subjects of pictures required were sometimes inserted in microscopic script in the margins. These may be very brief instructions – 'Job assis et tout nu', 'une bataille cruelle', both actual examples – or may actually describe the scenes in some detail. Iconography and symbolism were important in medieval art, and attributes of individual figures might need explaining fully if the artist did not have the exemplar in front of him or if the new manuscript was to be richer than its predecessor or somehow different in design. Marginal instructions are more common in literary or historical texts than in Books of Hours where subject matter was fairly standard: the Annunciation at Matins, the Visitation at Lauds, the Nativity at Prime and so on. Even in Books of Hours the odd guide word can be detected and written directions necessarily imply that the artist could read. Sometimes in manuscripts one still sees faint little sketches in the margins beside miniatures with thumbnail diagrams of the scenes. These may have been drawn by the scribe or stationer, or by the master artist outlining plans in conversation with an apprentice, or even by the artist himself thinking aloud while doodling with his plummet. It was obviously intended that marginal instructions and sketches should be erased when the finished manuscript was tidied up for binding, and they survive only by chance. Cleaning pages is often itemised in medieval accounts for bookbinding.

The rounded precise shape of the initial 'D' here was determined by the scribe who allowed appropriate space for it. (MS. Digby 20, fol. 194r, northern England (Durham), early twelfth century)

The technique of illuminating a manuscript is described frequently in medieval artists' manuals. Actually painting entirely in accordance with such written recipes is difficult and a certain care is needed in interpreting texts which may be primarily literary exercises rather than didactic instructions. Technique was presumably usually taught by practical example of master to apprentice or father to son rather than through written textbooks of self-improvement. Nonetheless, examination of unfinished manuscripts and an awareness of how manual writers claimed to operate can give us a reasonable insight into the stages of work.

Let us assume, as the writers do, that the artist and scribe were different people, and that the written gatherings had been delivered with spaces marked out for initials and illuminated miniatures. Probably the surface of the parchment would need to be given a final rubbing over with pumice or a concoction of powdered glass mixed in bread, and perhaps dusted off again with some kind of chalk to give it a really clean grease-free surface. The very rough design can be sketched out in the appropriate place in metalpoint and sometimes altered and corrected to achieve an acceptable composition for a miniature or a good flowing curve for an ivy-leaf border or a balanced geometric interlace. If a circle is part of the composition, one will expect to be able to detect the prick of a compass point showing through on the verso of the page. This sketch is very light. If done with charcoal or graphite it runs the risk of rough granules showing through into the final painting. The outlines are then rapidly completed in ink, 'crisping up' the composition, as Cennino's *Libro dell'Arte* says in the late fourteenth century. The Göttingen Model Book of around 1450 recommends that these outlines over metalpoint should be done in very thin ink or thin black colour, and that they should then be polished with a

The designs for illumination and miniatures were drawn first in ink, as seen here in an unfinished manuscript of the *Trionfi* of Petrarch. (MS. Canon. Ital. 83, fol. 9v, Italy (perhaps Ferrara), third quarter of the fifteenth century)

E se icostumi lor suspir ecanti
El parlar rocto el subito silentio
El breuissimo riso elungi pianti
E qualel mel temperato cõ lasentio .

O sciã che mia fortuna ĩforça altrui
Mebbe conducto etucti incisi mẽ
Delibertate oualcũ tempo fui
Io che era piu saluatico che ceruí
Racto dimesticato fui cõ tucti

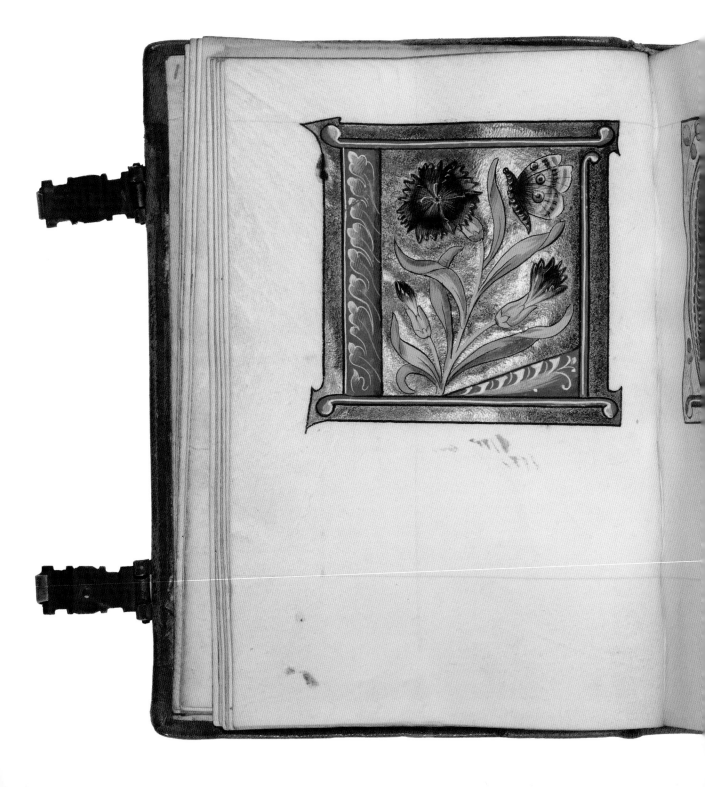

tooth to make them receptive to paint on top. It is quite surprising how sketchy these preliminary outlines can be in an illumination which will end up as high-quality work.

The actual designs of medieval miniatures were often copied from other sources. The details of exactly how this happened are elusive. The practice of taking an adaptable image in one manuscript and copying it into another goes back to the beginning of medieval book production. There is, for example, the frontispiece of the Codex Amiatinus, the great Bible copied out in Northumberland around AD 700, showing the Old Testament prophet Ezra writing beside an open book cupboard. The picture is almost certainly copied from one in a sixth-century Italian manuscript when the same scene with the same book cupboard represented Cassiodorus rather than Ezra. In turn, the same convenient image was then re-copied into the early eighth-century Lindisfarne Gospels where it now served as a portrait of the evangelist Matthew. An attractive picture seemed worth copying, even if it represented a different subject each time. There was no feeling, as we might have now, that slavish copying of images was somehow morally inappropriate. At the other end of the Middle Ages, the miniature of the Christ Child being brought to Simeon in the *Très Riches Heures* of the Duc de Berry, illuminated by the Limbourg brothers in France between about 1411 and 1416, is very closely copied, including elaborate architectural details, from part of the fresco by Taddeo Gaddi painted in Florence in 1328 illustrating the Virgin Mary as a young child being brought to the Temple. The remarkable representation of one scene has been taken out of context and transferred without inhibition into a manuscript. Obviously the Limbourgs did not sit down with the half-made *Très Riches Heures* and a set of paint pots in the chapel itself in Santa Croce in Florence but based their composition on a drawing or pattern sheet.

An illuminator's pattern book with sample letters of the alphabet suitable for manuscripts. (MS. Douce f. 2, fol. 12v, France, early sixteenth century)

Pattern books and specimens played an important part in producing the images in manuscripts. Several dozen medieval pattern books and model sheets survive, some comprising myriads of isolated pictures which could be copied into part of manuscript compositions or into any other form of pictorial art, and others which are specifically for manuscripts with samples of decorated initials or borders. The most common pictorial images from patterns are birds and animals, or human figures in different poses. Pictures of deer, lions, unicorns and herons, for example, recur almost identically incorporated into borders and miniatures of widely divergent manuscripts. By the middle of the fifteenth century patterns were being engraved, or engravings were being used as pattern sheets (this is not as clear as one would like), and images such as big roses and wildmen and a stag scratching its ear can be charted in manuscript designs right across northern Europe. Certain workshops evidently had their own patterns. There are compositions that are characteristic of individual artists and their workshops, especially in Paris from as early as about 1220. There was a lawsuit in 1398 in which the well-known illuminator Jacquemart de Hesdin was alleged to have led a robbery against the painter John of Holland and to have broken open his strongbox and stolen various paints and patterns. In Flemish manuscripts of around 1500 one finds the most uncanny duplication of miniatures from one manuscript to the next, with every detail mirrored. Books of Hours illuminated by Simon Bening or Gerard Horenbout in Bruges in the early sixteenth century can look so alike that it can be very difficult to distinguish between them.

Not enough is known about how this copying was done, and nothing about why it was done. One would have imagined that a competent miniaturist would have been capable of designing freehand. Yet there is good evidence that compositions of

A pattern book including images of a coney and a beaver. (MS. Ashmole 1504, fol. 31v, eastern England, first half of the sixteenth century)

Cone. Castor.

memorie cõmendate: hoc in
uia fide conscribite. Hoc autẽ
ut intelligatis: ad dñm patrẽ
& filium qui unũ sunt. pces
fundite. Explicit sermo. li. Incipit. lii. de ubrs dñi. in euãgdio
sedm iohm. Õm qui credit in eũ:
credit in illũ qui eum misit.

Hoc admonuit
dñs cum euuan-
gelium legeret:
qm qui credit
meum. credit in eũ qui illum
misit. Missum esse ad nos sal-
uatorẽ mundi. fides uerissima
tenet: qm xpm ipse pdicat
xpc: hoc est corp xpi. toto orbe diffusum. In celis enĩ ille erat:
& seruienti in terra psecutori dicebat. Quid me psequeris? Ybi
dñs sic expressit: & hic se esse
in nobis. Sic totus crescit: quia
sicut in nobis est hic. ita & nos

caput corp suum: & ido nc
mundus odit. sicut ab ipso
dño audiuim? Hon enĩ apl'
hoc dicebat paucis. qd odit
eos mundus: & quia gaudere
deberent cũ eis detraherent
hoies. & dicerent omia mala
aduersum eos: qa ppter hec. me-
ces eoru maior est in celis. Hon
eis solis dixit dñs. cũ hec dixit
s; dixit uniũso corpi suo: dix
omibz menbris suis. Quicũq;
in corpe ei. & de menbris ei est
uoluerit: ñ miretur. quia od
eum mundus. Corpis autem
sacramtcum. multi accipiun
s; ñ oms qui accipiunt sacra
mentum. habituri sunt apu
eum. etiã locum pmissu men
bris ei. Sacramtcum qdem p
oms. corpus ei dicunt: qa oms
mpascuts ei simul pascunt:
uenturus est qui diuidat:

miniatures could be literally traced from one copy to another using transparent *carta lustra* or *carta lucida*, or could be duplicated by 'pouncing' in which the outlines of the original were pricked with rows of holes and placed over the new page and dabbed with a bag of colour, such as charcoal dust, to produce a dotted outline. This would provide a sketchy outline, like the metalpoint drawings described above, ready to be strengthened in ink in preparation for colouring.

Some pictures or initials in medieval manuscripts are formed only of drawing, especially in the Carolingian and Romanesque periods or in some scientific or practical books, but most decoration was intended to be coloured and it was often illuminated. Strictly speaking, 'illumination' requires use of gold or silver which reflects the light. A manuscript with much decoration but in colours without actually having gold or silver is, technically, not illuminated. Members of the Cistercian Order were permitted to ornament their manuscripts but not to illuminate them, as gold was thought to be frivolous and inappropriate to an austere way of life. Illumination with gold goes back into antiquity but is especially common in the later Middle Ages. The occurrence of gold in manuscripts at different periods can be linked with changes or interruptions in trade routes from gold mines. Manuscripts such as Books of Hours are almost always illuminated. If gold leaf is to be applied to a design in a manuscript it is put on before the colour. This is crucial for two reasons. The first is that gold will adhere uninvited to any pigment which has already been laid, ruining the design, and secondly the action of burnishing it is vigorous and runs the risk of smudging any painting already in place around it.

There are several methods of applying gold to pages of manuscripts and sometimes more than one technique was used in a single miniature in order to achieve different effects. There are

Cistercian manuscripts were supposed to be decorated in monochrome, without gold, such as this copy of Saint Augustine from Meaux Abbey in Yorkshire. (MS. Rawl. C. 415, fol. 2v, England (Meaux), mid-twelfth century)

three basic types of application appropriate for books. Two methods use gold leaf, and one uses powdered gold. In the first a design is brushed on in some kind of wet glue and the gold leaf is laid on top and is burnished when it is dry. This is used particularly in very early manuscripts and it can achieve wonderful areas of shimmering gold like the backgrounds of early panel paintings. In the second method a sticky gesso is prepared and built up so that the design is really three-dimensional. When the gold has been applied and polished with a burnishing tool it looks extremely thick and the curving edges of the design catch the light from many angles at once. This is the most wonderful medieval gold in manuscripts and is discussed in more detail below. The third method is to apply what is called 'shell' gold, a powdered gold mixed with gum arabic into a kind of gold ink (and commonly dispensed from a sea shell such as a mussel or oyster, hence the name) and applied with pen or brush. It can also be called matt or liquid gold. Unlike leaf gold, it was added after the colour. It was particularly used from the second half of the fifteenth century, and can resemble the frosted gold printed on some old-fashioned Christmas cards. It is curious that it was so popular, because the effect (at least to modern eyes) can easily be sugary and overdone, it must have been more expensive to make since grinding up pieces of gold uses more of the material than laying leaf, and those who have tried highlighting in shell gold over pigment report that it is a slow process to apply scores of hatched lines with repeated precision.

Gold leaf is not especially easy to use either. It is a property of gold that, unlike many other metals, it can be hammered thinner and thinner without ever disintegrating into crumbs. A piece of gold leaf is infinitely thinner than the thinnest paper. It is virtually without thickness and has almost no weight. If rubbed between the finger and thumb it will fade into nothing. If dropped it hardly seems to flutter downwards. If it settles on a hard surface ruffled or folded it can be straightened out with a puff of breath, unwrinkling itself instantly like a shimmering shaken blanket. It can be eaten and seems to vanish on the tongue. Cennino recounts that goldbeaters could make 145 leaves of gold from hammering one gold ducat. It was comparatively rarely used in medieval manuscripts before about 1200, with certain royally lavish exceptions. This may be in part because until then many manuscript painters worked in monastic cloisters open to the wind. Trying to handle gold leaf in such conditions must have been fraught with frustration and wasted gold. But by the thirteenth century, when most work was probably conducted indoors, the manipulation of

Gold leaf, which can be hammered to almost no thickness and virtual weightlessness, was used a great deal in medieval illumination.

gold leaf was at least reasonably possible. Gold leaf is comparatively cheap, even now. Thus in Robert Brekeling's contract to make a manuscript in 1346 with gold initials throughout, the gold was accounted at 18d., less than a tenth of the overall cost. Cennino says that when buying gold leaf, 'get it from someone who is a good goldbeater; and examine the gold; and if you find it rippling and matt, like goat parchment, then consider it good'.

Both Cennino and the Göttingen Model Book describe at some length the mixing of gesso for raised illumination. Begin with slaked plaster of Paris, and grind in a little white lead (less than a third of the amount of the plaster, Cennino says). The mixture is very white and crumbly. The Göttingen manuscript takes up the recipe: 'then fetch *bolum armenum* at the apothecary's, and grind so much into it that the chalk will turn a red flesh colour therefrom'. Armenian bole, as it was called although it certainly came from many places closer than Armenia, is a kind of greasy red clay. It has no real function in gesso except to supply colour. When the gesso is eventually applied to the white page the inclusion of a colouring substance will make the mixture easier to see; and if the gold should ever wear off a bit, a pinky brown colour underneath gives a more pleasing and warmer glow than stark white. It is interesting to look out for traces of bole having been used in the illumination of manuscripts. Usually, especially in rather battered manuscripts, one can detect whether or not the gesso under the gold has been mixed with bole. In Italy it is pink. In Flanders and Germany it is brown. In Paris bole is usually not used at all. This must be one of those curious differences which, if enough examples could be systematically collected up and documented, might one day help localise manuscripts or at least the place of the illuminator's training.

However, to return to the recipe, we now have plaster and white lead, with or without colouring. Add a dash or two of sugar. Sugar, or honey for that matter, has the property of attracting moisture and it is important that the concoction should remain damp as long as possible. The mixture is now powdery, pink, sweet and poisonous. It is sensible to add a little gum, though the recipes do not call for it. The substance can be dried into little pink pellets and stored like this. When it is needed mix it up with a little clear water and egg glair, presumably on a slab of stone, crunching the mixture over and over with a palette knife until it is really smooth and runny, without bubbles. The egg glair is made from the sticky liquid which forms at the bottom of a bowl of whipped egg whites, especially if a cup of cold water is tipped in too.

This is gesso, a mixture which needs to be stirred often, ready for use. It is applied with a quill pen, not a brush. Speed is important, as is a lightness of touch so as not to scratch the parchment with the nib. The liquid is puddled into the centre of the piece to be gilded and then quite quickly drawn out carefully into the corners and over the parts of the manuscript page marked out by the underdrawing, round the shape of initials, into ivy leaves, haloes, dotted across tessellated chessboard backgrounds, and so on. When finished, the page looks as though it is covered with pink boils, blobby and thick. Presumably the medieval illuminator, unlike the scribe, worked at a flat table rather than at a sloping desk as the gesso is piled up thickly and held by surface tension and would run down a slope. It takes some time to dry. It is tempting to try to lay the gold too soon but this will only cause smudging.

Return next day. The gesso may have formed hollows in the middle as it dried, and if so it can be scraped smooth again with a knife. Damp weather or dank early mornings are said to be good for applying gold leaf. A fluttering piece of gold leaf is picked up on a thin flat brush called a gilder's tip and can be allowed to fall onto the soft gilder's cushion where it can (if appropriate) be blown out

LEFT: Modern technique of burnishing a gold initial.

flat and cut with a sharp knife into strips or other simple shapes before being picked up again on the brush. The illuminator breathes heavily onto the manuscript page and the dampness of his breath makes the gesso slightly tacky again, and the gold leaf can be lowered into place, overlapping the edges of the gesso pattern. As it nears the page the gold leaf seems to jump into place. It is covered quickly with a piece of silk or parchment and pushed quite firmly with the thumb. Patterns may be impressed from the weave of silk but they are of no consequence as they will be smoothed away in a moment. The illuminator then takes up the burnishing tool; this was traditionally a dog's tooth mounted on a handle, but Cennino says that the tooth of a lion, wolf, cat or any carnivore is as good, and he goes on to describe how to make a stone burnishing tool

RIGHT: Once the underdrawing was complete, the gold was added and burnished before any other colours were applied. (MS. Laud Misc. 322, fol. 4r, England, early fifteenth century)

Innocencius tercius papa de misera
bili humane condicionis egressu de con
temptu mundi et de unitis et diuisis alijs
condicionibz

E Egressus de uulua e
matris egressus
ut uiderem et labo
ren et consumere
tur dies mei in con
fusione: Si talia
locutus de se ille. quem dominus sanc
tificauit in utero: qualia loquar de me:
quem mater mea genuit in peccatis.
Heu me dixerim. mater quid me genu
isti filium. amaritudinis et doloris:
Quare non in uulua mortuus sum:
Egressus de utero non statim perij:
Cur exceptus genibus. uberibus lactar?
natus in conbustionem et cibum ig

ERE

DIGNV

& iustum est æquum

from a piece of hematite. The tool is rubbed up and down over and around the gold and into the crevices at its edge. As it rubs, the gold which generously overlapped the edges of the gesso design will fall away and these infinitely small crumbs of gold dust can be brushed off or swept up. If a page of a medieval illuminated manuscript is tipped to reflect light off the surface one can often see the marks of where the burnisher has overshot the design and pushed into the vellum. Obviously it was rubbed with pressure and speed. It is almost miraculous the way that a microscopically thin piece of gold will buff up into a really remarkable shine, even as one watches. The transformation is startling. It will never fade. Gold cannot tarnish. The burnished gold in manuscripts sparkles as new after five hundred or a thousand years. Silver, by contrast, oxidises and turns black and presents problems which medieval illuminators struggled to overcome, usually in vain.

Once the gold is in place, the rest of the decoration can be coloured. A number of twelfth-century English manuscripts evidently had the underdrawing marked out with tiny letters of the alphabet, 'a', 'r', 'v' and so on, to indicate the colours, *azure, rouge, vert* (unless it is Latin, *azura, rubeus, viridus*), as if the infilling was more or less painting by numbers. Quite often one has to assume that the underdrawing is by one artist and the colouring by another. The elaborate and to us rather patronising instructions on how to lay colours given in the Göttingen Model Book suggest that the completion of simple designs was a beginner's task. Paint the red. Then take a brush and outline it with darker red. Then dilute the dark red in a shell and lighten the red. Then take white and heighten the light red. These kind of directions for painting simple leaves run for many pages, colour after colour in the same order, as if addressing a child. A twelfth-century miniature in Prague does indeed show a child Everwinus painting manuscript ornaments

In early manuscripts gold was used on pages of extreme luxury, as in the Canon of the Mass in this Sacramentary illuminated in the Franco-Saxon style. (MS. Bodl. 579, fol. 6ov, northern France or Flanders, second half of the ninth century)

ruentir unus de septrem an
gelis qui habant phialas z
locutus est mecum dicens. Veni
ostendam tibi sponsam uxorem
agni. Et sustulit me in montem
magnum z altum. et ostendit m̄
ciuitatem sanctam ierlm descende
tem de celo a deo habentem clarita
tem dei. Lumen eius simile lapi
di pretioso tanquam lapis iaspi
dis simile cristallo. Et habebat z
murum magnum z altum ha
bens portas duodecim. Orienta
lem videlicet australem et aqui
lonem precepitq; deus ut porta z

orientalis clausa super maneret.
principe tantum modo per eam in
trante exeunte. Et in portis an
gulos duodecim. et nomina scrip
ta duodecim tribuum filiorum
ierlm. Ab oriente porte tres. z ab
aquilone porte tres. ab austro por
te tres. z ab occasu porte tres. Et
in ipsis scripta nomina duodeci
apostolorum agni. z cetera.

ruentir unus de septrem anglis
qui habant phialas. z locutus est
mecum dicens. veni ostendam ti
bi sponsam uxorem agni. et cetera

Superius in quinta uisione dicit iohannes.
septrem anglo hentes phialas se fuisse mostros.

The famous unfinished Douce Apocalypse shows the different stages of applying (and burnishing) the gold, and then gradually inserting the different colours. (MS. Douce 180, p. 92 and p. 76, England (probably Westminster), second half of the thirteenth century)

Q ui diuites facti sunt ab ea
longe stabunt propter timo
rem tormentorum eius flentes
et lugentes et dicentes. Ue. uea
uitas illa magna que amicta e
tat bisso et purpura et cocco et inaura
ta auro et lapide preciofo et mar
garitis. quoniam una hora destru
xerunt sunt tante diuicie. Et om
nis gubernator et omnes qui in
locum nauigant et naute qui in
mari operantur longe steterunt
et clamauerunt uidentes locum
incendii eius dicentes. Que fi
mul ciuitati huic magne et in

serunt puluerem super capita sua
flentes et lugentes et dicentes. Ue
ue ciuitas magna in qua diuites
facti sunt omnes qui habent na
ues in mari de preciis eius. quoni
am una hora desolata est. Exulta
super eam celum et sancti apostoli
et prophete. quia iudicauit deus iu
dicium uestrum de illa.

ui diuites facti sunt ab ea. et c̄.

Post tunus per mare hic seculum per gubernatores
uero principes iniquos intelligere. per eos autem q
de loco ad locum nauigant et per nautas qui in mari
operantur. eos qui diuersa officia ad depredationes
pauperum et ad peccata sua cotidie agenda immun
te exercent. Ista ergo flebunt et lugebunt uidentes
locum incendii babilonis. Ipsi namq̄ erunt babilo
et ipsi flebunt et lugebunt. Uidebunt autem incen
dia babilonis. quia sua incendia perferendo uidebit.

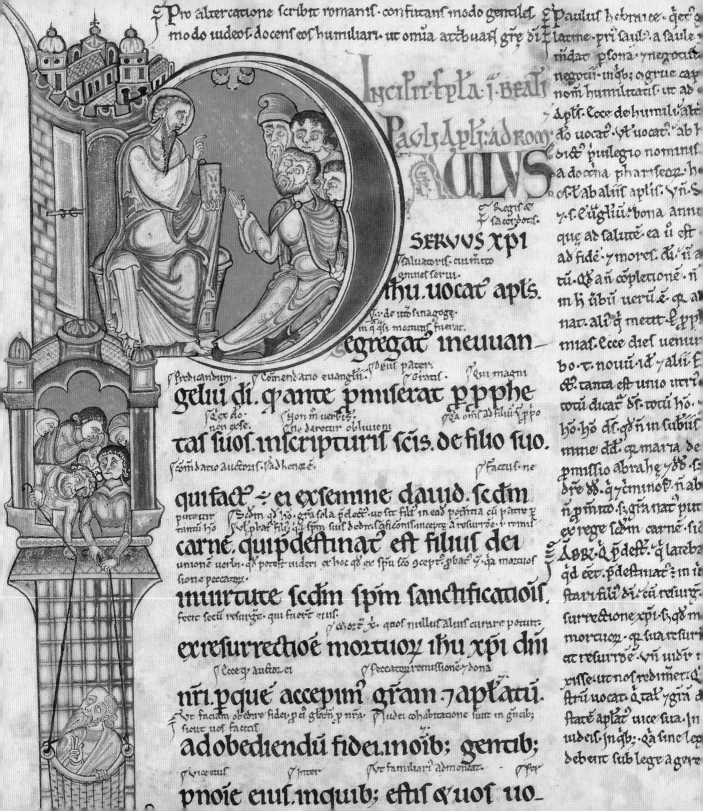

Incipit epla i beati
Pauli Apli ad rom...
AULUS

SERVUS XPI

thu. uocat apls.

egregat ineuuan

gelii di. qñ ante pmiserat p pphe

tas suos. inscripturis scis. de filio suo.

qui fact? e. ex semine dauid. scdm

carne. qui pdestinat? est filius dei

inuirtute scdm spm sanctificatiois.

ex resurrectioe mortuoy ihu xpi dñi

nri. pque accepim? grãm 7 apltatu

ad obediendu fidei. in noibus; gentibus;

ñ noie eius. inquibus; estis q uos uo

while his master, the scribe Hildebertus, shouts at a mouse stealing cheese. This is not to belittle the works of medieval manuscript painters by suggesting that all manuscripts were painted by children: far from it, for there are illuminated manuscripts by artists of the highest rank, including Perugino, Fouquet, Botticelli, Mantegna, Dürer, Holbein.

It is perhaps possible that the Göttingen Model Book instructions were not for any practical use at all but simply show (in the literary disguise of a primer) a scholar's analysis of how he believed decoration in a manuscript could have been executed. We too can gaze at manuscripts and detect simple sequences of applying the colour, one layer overlapping another. First the area is painted, then darkened for the shadows, and then lightened on the other side, and then finished with any delicate details of facial expression in dark colour and finally in white. Once again, unfinished manuscripts can show different stages. There is no especial trick to the technique of manuscript painting. It was executed much as anyone now would if attempting the same task. Genius stands out, and hack work can be very bad indeed.

Some modern scribes assert with the credibility of practical experience that a great deal of medieval manuscript decoration was executed with a pen rather than a brush. This may have been true, especially for flourished initials (for example) where the body of the infilling was in one colour without heightening. If the paint has rubbed thin, one can see penstrokes. The Göttingen instructions suggest both implements were used: 'you shall apply all colours, shade and heighten them, with a brush, except in the checkered backgrounds, which you shall apply with the pen and heighten with the brush; otherwise, all foliage and flower work with a brush, large or small'. There are sixteenth-century instructions for making brushes for portrait miniatures. Use clippings from

Occasionally tiny letters of the alphabet are still visible under areas of paint, indicating the designer's instructions of the colour to be added, as here 'v' (*vert*, green), 'a' (*azure*, blue) or 'r' (*rouge*, red). (MS. Auct. D. 1. 13, fol. 1r, England (possibly Winchester), mid-twelfth century)

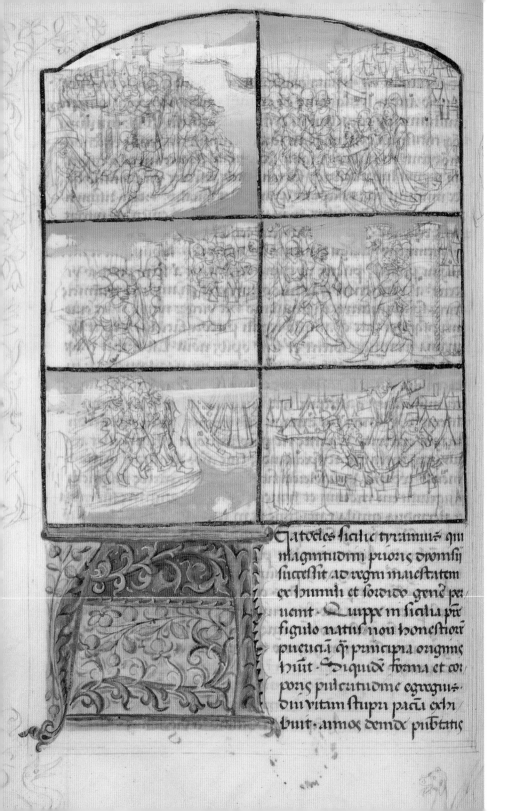

Gatocles sicilie tyrannus qui
magnitudini prioris dionisij
successit ad regni maiestatem
ex humili et sordido gene per=
uenit · Quippe in sicilia pre
figulo natus non honestiori
puericiã cp̃ principia origine
hñit · Siquidẽ forma et cor=
poris pulcritudine egregius
diu vitam stupri pactu exhi=
buit · annos deinde pubtatis

Colour was applied over the underdrawing in stages, often beginning with the backgrounds first, as here, in unfinished and completed miniatures from the same manuscript. (MS. Auct. F. 2. 29, fols. 71v and 15v, France, second half of the fifteenth century)

Nascitur in lutania mamo
rubicundis ornata cuiculis.
Herbā cruas bulliat cū
gen imponitur. summe
incorpore. Herbe
oms dolores sedat.

ris albi colorē habet. & quoquot
☞ SCIATICA
adipe apsino qsi malagma
facit.   ☞ OMS DOLORES
grias radix pissata & iposita

GRECIS DICITVR **Capilli ueneris**   Adiatos

A lii	Politricon
A lii	Tricomanens
A lii	Ebemaricon
Ægypti	Ethic
Romani	Cincinnalis
A lii	Terre capillus

the tail hairs of the miniver or the calaber (species of ermine and squirrel respectively) rolled up in strips of paper, tied and inserted into the end of a barrel of a feather. Thus it may be that pictures of illuminators apparently holding quills are in fact wielding brushes.

The range of colours available to the medieval manuscript painter was surprisingly large. Red, for example, could be made from minium (lead oxide) or from cinnabar (mercuric sulphide), found naturally in parts of Spain and Tuscany. Vermilion is an artificially manufactured variant of cinnabar, made from heating mercury with sulphur and then by collecting and grinding the deposits of vapour formed during the heating process. It is very poisonous, and so the old artist's trick of bringing a brush to a fine point by licking it was a calculated risk. Alternatively, red pigment can be made from plant extracts. Brazilwood has already been mentioned in connection with red ink. Madder, a rather purply red, is made from the root of the madder plant, which grows wild in Italy. A romantically named red, widely used in book decoration, was dragon's blood, described in medieval encyclopedias as a pigment formed not merely from dragons but from the mingling of the blood of elephants and dragons which have killed each other in battle. It actually comes from the sap of the shrub *Pterocarpus draco*.

Blue is the second most common colour in medieval manuscripts, after red. It was very often made from azurite, a blue stone rich in copper, found in many countries of Europe. Azurite is very hard, and has to be smashed and then rammed and ground patiently with mortar and pestle until it slowly and dustily turns to powder. Another blue, much more of a violet blue, was made from the seeds of the plant turnsole, now called *Crozophora*. But the blue prized above all others was ultramarine, blue from far beyond the sea, made from lapis lazuli, found naturally only in the mountains of Afghanistan (today it is available from Chile too, unknown in

One source of red pigment was the madder plant (*Rubia tinctorum*), here shown in an illustrated herbal. (MS. Bodl. 130, fol. 9r, England (Bury St Edmunds), late eleventh century)

the Middle Ages). The journey that this pigment must have taken to reach Europe is almost unimaginable, for it was available long before the time of Marco Polo, and it must have passed in bags from one camel train to another, to carts and ships, a medium of commerce over and over again, before finally being purchased at enormous expense from the apothecaries of northern Europe. Good blue paint was valuable. In the Winchester Psalter and the Dover Bible, both of the twelfth century, it was carefully scraped off for re-use. The inventory of the Duc de Berry, drawn up in 1401–3, includes among his treasures of unbelievable wealth two precious pots containing ultramarine.

Lapis is a dark blue stone excavated in the Himalayas and much prized as a pigment in the Middle Ages.

Other pigments included green from malachite (a copper carbonate) or from verdigris; yellow from orpiment (arsenic sulphide) or from saffron; white from white lead, and so on. There were several techniques of mixing pigments into paints. Both white of egg (egg glair) and yellow of egg (egg tempera) were common, egg being a very effective glue. Gums too were made from fish lime (the best was from the air bladder of the sturgeon) or from animal size made usually by boiling up pieces of skin. The grinding and the mixing and the tempering of paints were essential prerequisites to the decorating of illuminated manuscripts.

Presumably early medieval illuminators sat in the cloister like everyone else then engaged in book work. The self-portrait of Hugo Pictor, the late eleventh-century Norman painter, *'imago pictoris & illuminatoris huius operis'*, in a manuscript in the Bodleian Library, shows a tonsured cleric sitting in an armchair under an open architectural arch. His manuscript is to his right. Hugo is ruling his page with a knife in his right hand and with his left hand he dips a curved quill-like implement – it may still be a brush – into a horn in the arm of his chair. From over 400 years later, at the other end of our story, are two self-portraits by the renowned sixteenth-century Bruges illuminator Simon Bening (1483–1561). He was no monk; he married twice and had five legitimate children as well as an illegitimate daughter. In his portrait he is working indoors by the lattice window of a town house. The window is to the left of his desk, presumably so that light falling on his hand will not hide the detailed work in shadow. He holds his glasses (pictures of painters with spectacles are found as early as the fourteenth century) and wears a high smock, his hair held by a kind of black skull cap. The slightly later English miniaturist Nicholas Hilliard recommended the wearing of silk clothes while working, lest dust or hairs fall on the delicate wet paint, and keeping the head still for fear of

falling 'dandrawe of the head'. Shells of colours are ranged with other implements to the left of Bening's desk, next to the window.

Most medieval professional illuminators charged by the work, rather than by the hour. Generally labour was cheap and materials were expensive. Some of the earliest illuminated books from secular workshops, grand Bibles and luxury books made in and around Paris in the second half of the twelfth century, show one of a series of little marks in plummet beside each illuminated initial: one stroke, three strokes, a cross and so on. These seem to be related to the number of initials in each gathering, and are a calculation for payment. Illuminators' accounts were usually based on the number and size of the decorations, multiplied out. A thirteenth-century English glossed Gospel Book, for example, was supplied with red and blue initials and paragraph-marks at the cost of a penny for 300. There are, by my counting, just under 8,000 in the volume but the decorator gave a slight discount and charged 26d. One fifteenth-century English miscellany has three sizes of initial: big gold initials were charged at 4d. each; large painted initials were three for a penny; smaller paragraph marks were ten for a penny. In the Paston Letters there is an account for a Psalter decorated by Thomas Lympnour of Bury St Edmunds in 1467: full-page illuminations were 12d. each, half-page illuminations were 4d. each, small painted initials were 4d. a hundred, and capital letters were a penny a hundred. Here too is an exact sense of the hierarchy of decoration. The illumination alone came to £1.5s.10d.

The same book cost 12 shillings for binding. Seventy-five years earlier, Robert *bukebinder* charged York Minster 10 shillings for binding a Gradual for the choir, plus 20d. for four skins of parchment for flyleaves and 3s.2d. for a deerskin to cover the whole book. It was rather bigger than the Pastons' Psalter, and so the price is comparable. But the thirteenth-century glossed

The self-portrait of the manuscript illuminator Simon Bening of Bruges in 1558 (London, Victoria and Albert Museum, P. 139-1910, southern Netherlands, dated 1558)

manuscript, just cited, was not bound at all but sewn into wrappers, which cost a penny for sewing and a halfpenny for parchment. This was much cheaper.

The history of bookbinding is a long and intriguing subject in its own right. It is the last stage in producing a manuscript, however, and so it must end our story. A book was not yet ready for the customer when the artist had completed the illumination. It was still in loose gatherings and perhaps even dismembered further into separate pairs of leaves. These all had to be collected up, reassembled into order, and held together in some serviceable binding. In the late Middle Ages this would be the task of the stationer or bookseller and when a commercial bookbinder can be identified by name, he often proves to have been a stationer. This was the person who had taken the order for the manuscript in the first place and who had distributed the gatherings among the illuminators of the town. It was now the stationer's task to call in the various parts of the book, clean them up (erasing guide words and smudges left over from the various stages of manufacture), assemble them in sequence according to the signatures or catchwords, and to bind the book for the client. In the earlier Middle Ages, when books were mostly made by monks, the binding was carried out by whatever member of the community was able to do so. The Lindisfarne Gospels, according to a tenth-century inscription, had been bound by Bishop Æthelwald, 'as he well knew how to do'. Another bishop, Saint Osmund of Salisbury (d. 1099), is credited by William of Malmesbury with having bound manuscripts for the cathedral with his own hands. Quite often catalogues of monastic libraries include a shelf or two of unbound books, sometimes described as 'in quaternis', which presumably means stitched into some kind of wrappers rather than literally in loose quires.

Istud Volumen scriptum & compositum fuit opera Vespasiani. Librarij Florentini. Jnciuitate florentie de Año 1459.

From the earliest times when manuscripts were first made in book form, rather than as rolls or tablets, the gatherings were held together by sewing thread through the central fold. The earliest surviving Coptic bookbindings date from around the fourth century. They are held together by chain stitching, that is, with each gathering sewn through the centre and then linked around its spine to the next gathering which is stitched too and linked in sequence to the next, and so on. The book is a stack of gatherings joined one to another with the sewing of the first and last gatherings knotted into the covers. Greek and Oriental bindings were basically like this, and so were the earliest monastic bindings of western Europe. Ethiopian bindings still are, and a chest full of modern Ethiopian books looks much as the library of Jarrow must have looked in the eighth century with big square wobbly wooden bindings.

A note on the flyleaf of this Cicero records that the volume was written and assembled by the famous bookseller, Vespasiano da Bisticci, of Florence, in 1459. The assembly probably refers to the binding-up of the gatherings. (MS. Auct. F. 1. 12, fol. v verso, Italy (Florence), dated 1459)

Through most of the Middle Ages, however, manuscripts were sewn onto bands or thongs or cords running at right angles horizontally across the spine. The stitching of each gathering goes through the centre fold and around the band, through the centre fold again and out around the next band, back through the centre fold again, and so on. The next gathering is the same, and the next, and the next, until all the gatherings are attached securely to the thongs across their spines. From at least the twelfth century the stitching was done with the help of a sewing frame. This is a wooden contraption, rather like a gate, which stands upright on the bench. The bands for the spine are tied to it vertically, suspended from top and bottom of the frame. The first gathering of the manuscript is placed on the bench with its spine up against these taut bands and is sewn through its centre and around the bands. Then the next gathering is placed on top, tapped down with a block of wood to keep the result firm and tight, and sewn to and around the bands. It continues like this until all the book is there, lashed by its spine to the frame. Sewing is the most time-consuming part of bookbinding. Methods of actually stitching the gatherings varied from century to century and place to place, sometimes a herring-bone stitch, sometimes a kettle stitch, sometimes going round the band once, or twice round it, or through splits in the bands themselves, and other variants interesting for their own sake and for dating bindings but not altering the basic principle. When the sewing is complete, the bands can be untied from each end of the frame. The book may feel loose and swivel rather, and this can be tightened up (as it was in the later Middle Ages) by sewing on stout headbands along the top and bottom edge of the spine.

The boards of medieval manuscripts were generally made of wood. Oak was commonly used in England and France; beech was usual in Italy, or pine, and bound Italian manuscripts feel

A modern sewing frame showing the traditional method of sewing the gatherings of manuscripts to cords which will be laced into the boards of the binding.

lighter than northern books. Occasionally the boards were made of leather. The use of pasteboards (a kind of cardboard formed of layers of waste paper or parchment glued together), can be followed infrequently through the Middle Ages and from the late fourteenth century became more and more common in southern Europe, in Spain and into Italy in Bologna, Milan, and later Padua. Pasteboards were clearly manufactured in the binder's own workshop, for sometimes the second-hand paper used is found to comprise pieces of the bindery's accounts. The boards, of whatever material, were

A twelfth-century manuscript of Saint Gregory in a tawed leather binding over wooden boards, with an added label recording its presentation by Edward IV, king of England (d. 1483), to the royal chapel in Windsor. (MS. Bodl. 192, England, third quarter of the fifteenth century)

The board of this Anglo-Saxon manuscript was used twice, and shows the original cords from the early eleventh century and, when it was removed and reversed, the later medieval leather thongs pegged into the wood. (MS. Auct. F. 1. 15, inside lower board, England (Canterbury), early eleventh century)

squared up into the shape of the book. In earlier manuscripts the boards were cut flush with the edges of the pages; after about 1200 they began to project beyond the edges and were often bevelled on their edges. The bands on the back of the sewn gatherings were threaded into the boards. Frequently some kinds of flyleaves were added at each end of the book (these explain the cost of extra vellum in bookbinders' bills), sometimes reusing waste leaves of earlier and obsolete manuscripts, which can be unexpectedly fascinating now. The bands were attached into the boards by several methods, varying with time and place, but the basic method is the same. The ends of the bands were secured into the boards by hammering in wooden pegs or, sometimes in Italy, with nails. The manuscript is now within plain boards, and was usable left like this. The inventory made in 1481 of the private library of Jean Bayart, late canon of Courtrai, included 120 books of which forty-six were simply 'in asseribus', in boards.

Usually, however, the outside of the book was covered with leather, tawed or tanned, and sometimes dyed. A few Carolingian bookbindings have simple stamped patterns on the leather. There was a brief fashion for stamped bindings in northern France in the twelfth century and bindings ornamented with little tools exist (but are unusual) from the thirteenth and fourteenth centuries. Then around 1450 the practice became much more common. Sides of bindings from then on were frequently ornamented with repeated impressions of floral or animal devices. This is done with a metal tool on a wooden handle. The tool is heated. The binder grasps the handle in both hands and leans over the binding and pushes down, holding the handle close to his chest and chin, rocking slightly one way and then the other, and then lifts the tool quickly up. No great pressure is needed to leave a neat crisp blind impression. These were arranged in rows, or in lattice or

The earliest 'Romanesque' blind-stamped bindings are generally ascribed to Paris, like this example once at Admont Abbey in Austria. (MS. Broxbourne 83.1, France (probably Paris), second quarter of the twelfth century)

other patterns. The outside of the binding was often fitted then with metal bosses or protective corner-pieces, and usually with some kind of clasp to hold the book shut. Folded parchment, however well creased, is springy and inclined to cockle in varying temperatures and states of humidity unless it is held securely shut by the gentle pressure of clasps.

Medieval books were sometimes enclosed further in loose jackets, called chemises, which wrap around the fore-edge and keep out the dust. Far more frequently than the surviving medieval bindings suggest, manuscripts may have been covered with textiles and brocades (which have mostly long-since perished) or with precious metals and jewels (which have mostly been removed with motives of varying legitimacy) or with enamels or paintings. Medieval inventories often describe bindings, since the outside of a book is a simple guide to its recognition, and give the impression that the private libraries of rich men or the treasuries of great churches were filled with multicoloured and precious bindings. The craftsmanship of such bindings takes us beyond the work of the stationer and into the shops of the jeweller or enameller. It is always worth glancing at the fore-edge of a medieval manuscript. Usually the edges of the pages are planed off every time a book is rebound, but the fore-edge is sometimes missed and it is occasionally possible to see traces of original painted designs on the very edges of the leaves. Even if the binding itself is much later, one can sometimes dimly make out a shadow of what was evidently once a polychrome book, decorated on every side. The outsides of medieval manuscripts have changed, probably, much more than their insides.

This story has taken us from the cows and sheep in the meadows, from which the parchmenter worked, through the whole business of scribes ruling and quill-cutting and copying. It has

A decorated and incised binding of a manuscript chronicle with metal fittings and clasps. MS. Douce 367, upper cover (south Germany (Nuremberg), third quarter of the fifteenth century)

ar:

sic;

minum xp

uius

uar

tus a

gen

nt in

nec

mar

q: pec

stiterunt

o ius

& principes

BELOW: A chemise of white leather wrapped around and enclosing the binding of a Psalter commentary, probably from Eynsham Abbey, with its medieval title-label nailed to the lower cover. (MS. Bodl. 700, England, early thirteenth century)

LEFT: King David shown in this detail from a Psalter is holding a book apparently attached to a 'chemise' cover of soft leather or textile. (MS. Ashmole 1525, fol. 6r, England (Canterbury), early thirteenth century)

seen ingredients from trees and shrubs, insects, birds, animals and mountainsides all over Europe and imported along the trade routes from far beyond Europe. It has taken in the transcription and the preservation of all ancient and medieval learning and literature by churchmen and laity. It has looked at the craft of the illuminator as it was in the time of most of our ancestors for a thousand years. And it has ended up again with the cows and sheep whose skins the bookbinder used to cover medieval manuscripts which still exist in their hundreds of thousands.

The original silver-gilt binding of an illuminated Gospel Book inset with a slightly earlier ivory plaque. (MS. Douce 292, southern Netherlands (Liège), second half of the eleventh century).

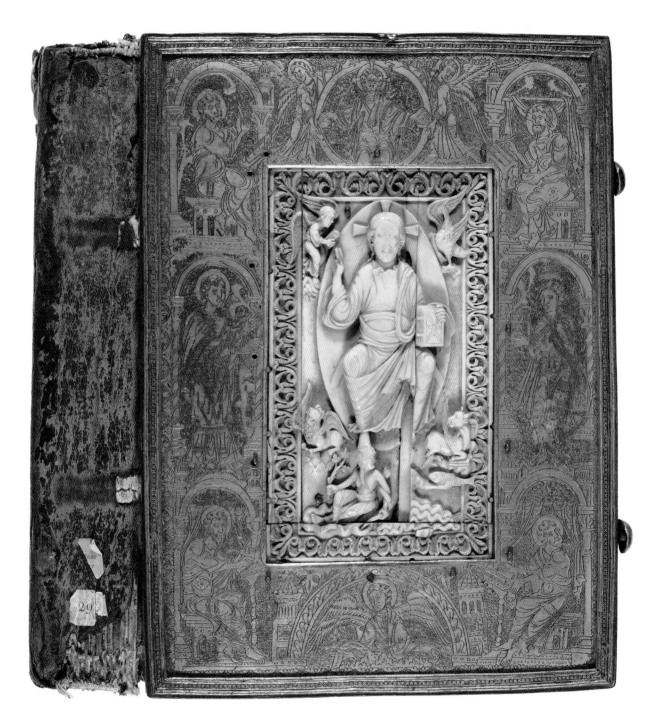

Amiral fu encoste
ses garde as fenestres
Et vit tant paueillons
vers ⁊ indes ⁊ bles
Estes vous vne espie qui vint deuers les gres
Qui dist que alixand' est en gibier remes
De cha gardent les tentes danclins ⁊ tholomes
Licanor ⁊ filote perdicas aristes
Li amiraus enuire ses lois ⁊ ses des
Ains que li rois reuiegne les assaudra as tres
⁊ copera les cordes sen sachera les pes
⁊ metra ⁊tre terre ⁊ forches ⁊ festes
Tout droit alamiral enuinrent li baron
Si li ont demande sire quel la feron
Entresi quala porte vienent lor paueillon
Faites la nous ouurir ⁊ si nous en istron
Lamiral respondi par ma foi non feron
Ces ichi deuant tholomer ⁊ cliton
⁊ sont ensamble o euls li xij. gpaignon
Se croure me uoles par decha ieron
Se nous ouurons la porte iames ne la clozron
Ains serions tuit pris par itele achoison
Si home li respondent bien est si lotroion
Lamiral sen issi o merueilleuse gent
Qui la reude de pie itant celement
Que nus qui fust en lost nen sot onques noient

GLOSSARY

Bifolium Two leaves (four pages) formed of a single folded sheet of vellum or paper.

Book of Hours A lay person's prayerbook containing prayers and psalms to be said at different times of the day.

Burnishing tool Tool used to polish gold once it has been applied to the manuscript page.

Catchword Words written by the scribe in the lower margin of the last page of a gathering repeating those at the top of the next page, as an aid to the binder to keep the gatherings in order.

Codex Manuscript volume.

Egg glair White of an egg used as an adhesive in mixing pigments into paints.

Egg tempera A paint which uses egg as an adhesive.

Gathering Folded section of vellum or paper leaves which could be bound together with other gatherings to form a book.

Gesso Plaster-like ground used for raised illumination.

Gloss Commentary or interpretation or quotation from a recognised authority added in the margins of a manuscript or between the lines of text.

Lunellum Crescent-shaped knife for scraping skin during the preparation of parchment.

Plummet A piece of lead used for ruling a parchment page.

Pouncing Duplication of pictures by pricking holes around their outlines and then rubbing pounce over them to reproduce a dotted outline on a sheet beneath.

Quire Gathering (q.v.).

Scriptorium Room set apart for writing, especially in a monastery.

'Shell' gold Powdered gold mixed with gum arabic into a kind of gold ink, and applied with a pen or brush.

Signature Gathering (q.v.).

Watermark Distinguishing mark or design on paper, made when the paper is in a pulp form, visible only when held up to the light.

Detail from MS. Bodl. 264,
fol. 84r, Flanders, completed
in 1344.

SELECT BIBLIOGRAPHY

J. J. G. Alexander, *Medieval Illuminators and their Methods of Work*, New Haven and London, 1992

B. Bischoff, *Latin Palaeography, Antiquity and the Middle Ages*, trans. D. Ó. Crónín and D. Ganz, Cambridge, 1990

M. Bollati, ed., *Dizionario biografico dei miniatori italiani secoli IX–XVI*, Milan, 2004

S. Bucklow, *The Alchemy of Paint: Art, Science and Secrets from the Middle Ages*, London, 2009

C. F. Bühler, *The Fifteenth-Century Book: The Scribes, the Printers, the Decorators*, Philadelphia, 1960

Cennino d'Andrea Cennini, *The Craftsman's Handbook, 'Il Libro dell' Arte'*, trans. D. V. Thompson, New Haven, 1933

H. Child, ed., *The Calligrapher's Handbook*, London, 1985

C. P. Christianson, *A Directory of London Stationers and Book Artisans*, 1300–1500, New York, 1990

M. Clarke, *The Art of All Colours: Mediaeval Recipe Books for Painters and Illuminators*, London, 2001

L. M. J. Delaissé, 'Towards a History of the Medieval Book', in *Codicologica*, I, *Théories et principes*, ed. J. P. Gumbert and M. J. M. De Haan, Leiden, 1976, pp. 27–39

A. Derolez, *Codicologie des manuscrits en écriture humanistique sur parchemin*, Turnhout, 1984 (*Bibliologia, Elementa ad Librorum Studia Pertinentia*, 5–6)

C. R. Dodwell, ed. and trans., *Theophilus, The Various Arts, De Diversis Artibus*, Oxford, 1961

M. Drogin, *Medieval Calligraphy: Its History and Technique*, Montclair and London, 1980

J. D. Farquhar, *Creation and Imitation: The Work of a Fifteenth-Century Manuscript Illuminator*, Fort Lauderdale, 1976

L. Gilissen, *Prolégomènes à la codicologie*, Ghent, 1977

M. Gullick, *Pen in Hand: Medieval Scribal Portraits, Colophons and Tools*, Walkern, 2006

D. Hunter, *Papermaking: The History and Technique of an Ancient Craft*, 2 ed., New York, 1947

E. Johnston, *Writing & Illuminating & Lettering*, London, 1906

H. Lehmann-Haupt, *The Göttingen Model Book: A Facsimile Edition and Translations of a Fifteenth-Century Illuminators' Manual*, Columbia, 1972

J. Murrell, *The Way How to Lymne: Tudor Miniatures Observed*, London, 1983

S. Panayotova, with D. Jackson and P. Ricciardi, eds., *Colour, The Art and Science of Illuminated Manuscripts*, London and Turnhout, 2016.

R. Reed, *Ancient Skins, Parchments and Leathers*, London and New York, 1972

R. Rouse and M. Rouse, *Manuscripts and their Makers: Commercial Book Producers in Medieval Paris, 1200–1500*, London and Turnhout, 2000

D. V. Thompson, *The Materials and Techniques of Medieval Painting*, New York, 1956

W. Wattenbach, *Das Schriftwesen im Mittelalter*, 3 ed., Leipzig, 1896

ACKNOWLEDGEMENTS

This book is an updated version of my *Scribes and Illuminators*, originally published by The British Museum Press in 1992 as part of their *Medieval Craftsmen* series. That publication, in turn, drew many observations from notes I had taken at a symposium convened by Chris Clarkson at West Dean College in 1990 on the practical techniques of making manuscripts. The occasion had included a demonstration of parchment-making by Wim Visscher, then of William Cowley Parchment Works in Newport Pagnell. I have also benefited then and on many other occasions since from countless conversations with practising scribes and illuminators, including Donald Jackson, Brody Neuenschwander (who showed me how to lay gold leaf, much harder than it looks when he does it), Patricia Lovett, Mark Van Stone, Michael Gullick and Scott Schwartz. I have enormous respect for those who have the skill to prepare parchment, cut quills, mix pigments and make manuscripts. If I have failed to understand my teachers, or if conclusions I drew are not necessarily applicable to all of the Middle Ages, I can only urge readers to conduct their own experiments and to examine original manuscripts. I shall be glad to receive ideas and corrections. There are many discoveries still to be made. Finally, I am delighted that this book has been brought back to life by the Bodleian Library in Oxford, where I spent several engrossing years as a graduate student in the early 1970s under the supervision of Richard Hunt, Keeper of Western Manuscripts. His advice was always to look at manuscripts, and to look and look again.

PICTURE CREDITS

INDEX

Illustrations are in *italic* page numbers and glossary words are in **bold.**

The scribe Ralph de Medylton, a self-portrait in a manuscript on the Passion of Christ. (MS. Bodl. 758, fol. 87r, England (Ingham, Norfolk), dated 1405)

...perimento cognouim̄. ex littal ba/
bemus. eosq̄ nouimus deo amabilis
impator. quia cum pauci quidam
buic fidi contradicant p̄iudicium
face non potuerunt. in toto orbe ter/
rarum. Multo enim tempe ab
berese arriana pulsati. nunc etiā
pietati contentione maxima con
tradicunt. Ut uero bec pietas tua
cognoscat. licet sciat tamen studui
imus fidem concilio niceno p̄fessam
ab epis trecentis decemq̄ octo subnun/
gere. Est autem bec niceni concilii
fides.

Credimus in unum deum pa/
trem omnip̄m. omnium uisibili
um inuisibiliumq̄ factorem. Et
in unum dñm ihm xp̄m filium
dei natum ex patre unigenitum
boc e de substantia patris. deum
de deo. lumen de lumine. dñm ue/
rum. de deo uero. natum nō factum.
consubstantialem patri. per quem
omnia facta sunt que in celo ex que
in tra. qui p̄pter nos homines z ppt
nr̄am salutem descendit incarnat.
humanatus. passus est: ex i die

bilem aut mutabilem filium dei:
bos anatematizat sca catholica ex
aplica eccla.

In hac fide deo amabilis impator
nos consistere necessarium e: tanq̄m
sacra ex aplica eccla: nulla q̄ moue
re eam seductione uerborum atq̄
contentione. quod abinitio arria
ni fecerunt. ex non extantibz filiū
dicentes: Non enim simpliciter si
milem dixerunt filium patri. ne sim
pliciter similis deo deus uerus ee
crederetur: z etiam consubstantialē
scpserunt. quod ipsum e genuini
ueriq̄ filii ex uero z naturali pre
nascentis. Sz neq̄ spm scm alie
nauerunt a pre ex filio. sz poti glfi
cauerunt eum cum patre ex filio:
in una sca trinitatis fide. eo quod
una sit in sca trinitate diuinitas.

As litteras impator legens: con
firmauit quam babuerat
de sacs scientiam ex affectum. ali
amq̄ consepsit legem. ut frume
torum consuetudo redderetur ecclis.
quam maximus distribuerat con
stantinus. ex dari pbibuerat iu

perimento cognouim̄. & littas habemus. eosq̄: nouimus deo amabilis impator. quia cum pauci quidam huic fidei contradicant p̄iudicium facere non potuerunt. in toto orbe terrarum. Multo enim tempe ab herese arriana pulsati. nunc etiam pietati contentione maxima contradicunt. Vt uero hec pietas tua cognoscat. licet sciat tamen studuimus fidem cilio niceno p̄fessam ab ep̄is tricentis decemq̄ octo subnungere. Est autem hec nicem cilii fides.

Credimus in unum deum patrem o̅ip̅m. omniu uisibilium inuisibiliumq̄: factorem. Et in unum d̅n̅m ih̅m x̅p̅m filium dei natum ex patre unigenitum hoc e̅ de substantia patris. deum de deo. lumen de lumine. d̅m uerum. de deo uero. natum n̅ factum. consubstantialem patri. per quem omnia facta sunt que in celo & que intra. qui p̄ter nos homines & p̄p n̅ram salutem descendit incarnat̄. humanatus. passus est: & i die

bilem aut mutabilem filium dei? hos anatematizat s̅c̅a catholica & ap̅lica eccl̅a. In hac fide d̅o amabilis impator nos c̅sistere necessarium e̅: tanq̄m sacra & ap̅lica eccl̅a: nulla q̄: moueri eam seductione uerborum atq̄: contentione. quod ab initio arriani fecerunt. ex non extantib̄: filiu dicentes? Non enim simpliciter similem dixerunt filium patri. ne si̅pliciter similis deo deus uerus e̅ crederetur? s; etiam co̅substantiale̅ sc̅pserunt. quod ip̄m e̅ genuini ueriq̄: filii ex uero & naturali p̄re nascentis. S; neq̄: sp̅m sc̅m alienauerunt a p̄re & filio. s; pot̄ gl̅ificauerunt eum cum patre & filio: in una sc̅e t̅rinitatis fide. eo quod una sit in sc̅a t̅rinitate diuinitas. As l̅ras impator legens? confirmauit quam habuerat de sc̅is scientiam & affectum. aliamq̄: consc̅psit legem. ut frumentorum consuetudo redderetur ecl̅is: quam maximus distribuerat constantinus. & dari pl̅ibuerat in